The Way of Water

and

Sprouts of Virtue

SUNY Series in
Chinese Philosophy and Culture

David L. Hall and Roger T. Ames, Editors

The Way of Water
and
Sprouts of Virtue

Sarah Allan

STATE UNIVERSITY OF NEW YORK PRESS

Cover illustration: Ten Views of a Thatched Lodge, Dong Qichang, (1555–1636) after Lu Hong (active ca. 713–741). *Courtesy National Palace Museum, Taipei, Taiwan, R.O.C.*

Production by Ruth Fisher
Marketing by Fran Keneston

Published by
State University of New York Press, Albany

For information, address the State University of New York Press,
State University Plaza, Albany, NY 12246

Library of Congress Cataloging-in-Publication Data

Allan, Sarah,
    The way of water and sprouts of virtue   /   Sarah Allan.
        p.   cm. — (Suny series in Chinese philosophy and culture)
    Includes bibliographical references and index.
    ISBN 0-7914-3385-4 (hardcover : acid free paper). — ISBN
0-7914-3386-2 (pbk. : acid free paper)
    1. Philosophy, Chinese.   2. Philosophy of nature.   I. Title.
II. Series.
    B126.A45   1997
    181'.11—dc20   96-36341
                                                                CIP

10 9 8 7 6 5 4 3 2 1

To Nicol Allan
Et maintenant, revenons à ces moutons.

Contents

Illustrations

Preface

This book is an exploration of the root metaphors of early Chinese philosophical thought. It is both an explication of certain early Chinese philosophical ideas and an investigation into the relationship between language and thought. The texts with which I will be concerned herein were written from the fifth to third centuries B.C., the golden age of Chinese philosophy. They include the *Analects* of Confucius, the *Laozi Daodejing*, the *Mencius*, the *Zhuangzi*, and the *Xunzi*. These works were cultural touchstones for all later Chinese civilization.

Written two and a half millennia ago in a language that has no genetic relationship to our own, the distance between the language and thought of these works and that of twentieth-century Europe and America could hardly be greater. On the one hand, they are proof of the universality of the human mind: they are understandable, at least in a general sense. We can learn to read them in the original and they can be translated into European languages. Once translated, they are not only comprehensible, but meaningful, and even speak of things in ways that we can apply to our own lives. Indeed, the *Laozi Daodejing* and the *Zhuangzi* are extraordinarily popular works throughout the world today. On the other hand, the texts are evidence of the richness of human diversity. Our understanding of them, especially when we approach them through the medium of our own language and culture, is both partial and inaccurate.

One reason that these texts are so readily accessible to us is that they are secular. Ancient China had no religious canon, no sacred narrative. Indeed, my thesis in this work is that in the absence of a transcendental concept, the ancient Chinese turned directly to the natural world—to water and the plant life that it nourishes—for the root metaphors of their philosophical concepts. Their approach was a holistic one: by studying the principles of nature, one could understand the forces that govern human society. Thus, in formulating the abstract principles of philosophical discourse, they took their models from natural phenomenon.

In recent years, as Western philosophers have become increasingly aware of the particularity of their own tradition and the shakiness of many of its foundations, many scholars have turned to China as a means of opening up, of seeking new questions and different answers. In so doing, however, they have tended to recast Chinese philosophy in the abstract technical terminology of European philosophical discourse. Even translation obscures many of the differences between Chinese and Western thought. Recast in this manner, the Chinese seem to be debating the same questions, though sometimes providing different answers.

This study is a concrete one. It begins with imagery rather than abstract concepts and attempts to rebuild—to reconstruct rather than deconstruct—the structure of early Chinese philosophical thought on the basis of its metaphoric models. By exploring the physical imagery implicit in some of the fundamental concepts of early Chinese philosophical thought, we begin to comprehend the connotations and potential range of meaning of these concepts as well as how they relate to one another structurally. Having established their structural relationships, we can also begin to understand more clearly what particular philosophers were saying about particular problems.

This is not a comparative study. Nevertheless, the very exercise of trying to think through another system of thought, to structure our thinking in an unaccustomed manner, abandoning many of our preconceptions, should allow us to gain some perspective on our own conceptual scheme, which is no less a product of historical and cultural circumstance than that of the ancient Chinese.

Acknowledgments

This work represents the culmination of the twenty-three years I taught at the School of Oriental and African Studies (SOAS), University of London. I completed its first draft in the Spring of 1995, just before I resigned to take up my present post at Dartmouth College. It is the product of teaching Chinese philosophical texts to SOAS students and also of the unique intellectual environment that once prevailed there. Thus I would like to take this opportunity to acknowledge some more intangible debts than those usually mentioned in these pages.

When I began teaching at SOAS in 1972, my most immediate colleagues were three of the finest sinologists in the Western world: D. C. Lau, A. C. Graham, and Paul Thompson. Lau, who invited me to SOAS when I was still finishing my doctoral dissertation, had an infectious enthusiasm for Chinese philosophy, including texts and problems that other people might consider dry as dust. I remember especially a period when he was reading the *Li Ji* (*Record of the Rites*) on the underground every morning and would recount his findings later in the day. For me, he will always be the embodiment of a Confucian gentleman. Angus Graham was Lau's Daoist counterpart, the pure intellectual, utterly unaware—or at least unwilling to take cognizance—of social convention, Chinese or Western. Although I did no more than briefly mention the idea for this book to him at the end of his life, his influence on my thinking will be obvious to anyone acquainted with his work. Paul Thompson is one of the most learned scholars I have ever met, and the most gracious person.

The forum for our discussions was occasionally the classroom, sometimes the senior common room, but more often the SOAS bar. There we were joined by succeeding generations of SOAS students, visiting scholars, and, indeed, anyone else who liked to talk and drink. They included such scholars as Roger Ames, Harold Roth, Henry Rosemont, Jean-Paul Reding, Christoph Harbsmeier, Charles D'Orban, and many others. I am also indebted to more recent SOAS students, including Wang Tao and Gillian Simpson whose critique of the first draft of this book was especially helpful to me.

Even more recently, Peter Rushton, Robert Henricks and Pamela Crossley, here at Dartmouth, and the SUNY readers, most importantly Constance Cook, have read and commented on the manuscript. I would also like to thank Neil Resnick for his help in compiling the indexes.

With the exception of the passage with which I open this work, the translations herein are my own. Nevertheless, I have read D. C. Lau's translations of the *Analects* of Confucius, the *Mencius*, and the *Laozi* [*Lao-tzu Tao Te Ching*] and A. C. Graham's translation of the *Zhuangzi* [*Chuang-tzu*] so often that my translations are inevitably indebted to theirs.

Finally, my most intangible, but most important, debt is to my husband, Nicol Allan. He has read and commented on numerous drafts of the manuscript with great care and patience and made many useful suggestions. I began to study Chinese in the same year that I married and he has always been the principal inspiration of my work. With this book, which is intended to be read by a nonspecialist as well as a sinological audience, my debt is even greater than usual.

Chapter 1

Introduction

The deepest satisfaction was in working one's way
inside a conceptual scheme so remote from our own,
the focus of attention always on distinctions rather
than resemblances, distinctions sometimes deep in
the structures of the Chinese and Indo-European
languages, and in discovering how they undermine
one's own presuppositions.
—A. C. Graham, *Reason within Unreason*

Figure 1. Listening to the Sounds of Spring under Bamboo, by Qiu Ying, Ming Dynasty (1368–1644). *National Palace Museum, Taipei, Taiwan, Republic of China.*

The following passage from D. C. Lau's translation of the Confucian philosopher *Mencius* is likely to convince even the most sympathetic Westerner of the inscrutability of the Chinese:

> Xuzi said, "More than once Confucius expressed his admiration for water saying, 'Water! Oh, water!' What was it he saw in water?" "Water from an ample source," said Mencius, "comes tumbling down, day and night without ceasing, going forward only after all the hollows are filled, and then draining into the sea. Anything that has an ample source is like this. What Confucius saw in water is just this and nothing more. If a thing has no source, it is like rain water that collects after a downpour in the seventh and eighth months. It may fill all the gutters, but we can stand and wait for it to dry up. Thus a gentleman is ashamed of an exaggerated reputation." (IVB.18)[1]

Although no translation into English of a text originally written in Classical Chinese can fully convey its meaning, the difficulty that the reader confronts in reading this passage is not due to the translation, but to a lack of familiarity with the imagery and to the strangeness of the assertion that Confucius frequently praised water. Indeed, few teachers can have tried to read this passage in a translation class, with Confucius' exclamation, *Shui zai! Shui zai!* 水哉! 水哉! "Oh Water! Oh Water." (Or perhaps, more evocatively, Ah, Water! Ah, Water![2]) without producing incredulity or even bemused laughter.

The contrasting imagery in this passage—water that falls in torrents but dries up in the sun as opposed to water that flows from a source, forever replacing itself—derives from a universal natural phenomenon and is readily understood with explanation or even a little thought. Confucius' stated admiration for water and the structure of the narrative, however, are more puzzling. Confucius did not understand reputation and then use water without a source as an analogy to illustrate the shame inherent in possessing an exaggerated reputation. He praised water and then derived a principle (*qu* 取) from it. From this principle—that things which have no source will dry up—he knew that a gentleman is ashamed when his reputation is greater than he is himself. Confucius' interest in water was not unique to him. Water is as important in the Daoist texts as in the Confucian. Indeed, water imagery is so pervasive in the *Laozi Daodejing* that scholars usually associate water imagery with the Daoist tradition rather than the Confucian.

Many scholars have observed that the Chinese religious tradition, unlike the ancient Greek and Judeo-Christian, did not assume a transcendent being or principle.[3] Nor did the Chinese have a sacred narrative, such as the Bible. That there is a close relationship between the root metaphors of the Indo-European religious traditions and the ontology of Western philosophy is well recognized. The root metaphors of Chinese thought, on the other hand, are much less obvious. In the following work, I will argue that early Chinese thinkers, whatever their philosophical school, assumed that common principles informed the natural and human worlds. By studying nature, one could understand humankind. Thus, the natural world rather than religious mythology provided the root metaphors for the formulation of many of the earliest Chinese philosophical concepts.

Water, which provides life, gurgles up unbidden from the earth and moves of its own accord, becomes perfectly level and clears itself of sediment when still, takes the shape of any container, penetrates the tiniest opening, yields to pressure but wears down the hardest stone, becomes hard as ice and disperses as steam, was the model for philosophical ideas about the nature of the cosmos. Plants, which germinate, grow until they blossom, and wither once they have produced seed, which thrive in the summer and die down in the winter, provided imagery for understanding the nature of man. This natural world was the source of the root metaphors used in the formulation of abstract concepts and its imagery is embedded in the language and structure of Chinese philosophy.

Water, with its multiplicity of forms and extraordinary capacity for generating imagery, provided the primary model for conceptualizing general cosmic principles, principles which applied to the behavior of people, as well as to the forces of nature. Plants—which water nourishes—served as a root metaphor for

4

understanding the nature of specific living things, including human nature. The Indo-European tradition makes a radical distinction between plants and animals. In English, for example, there is no common word that encompasses both plants and animals. In Chinese, however, people were included among the "myriad living things" (*wan wu* 萬物)—a category that encompassed both plants and animals. Such categories are fundamental to the way we think.

By exposing the metaphoric structures that are implicit in the language of Chinese philosophical discourse, we reveal the organization and internal relationships of its terms and categories. Thus, we begin to acquire a means of structuring our own thought in a manner that more closely resembles that of the ancient Chinese. This effort can never be entirely successful, especially when we are using the medium of another language, but it should allow our imaginations to glimpse the possibility of seeing the world in another way. And although the revelation may still be limited, it should nevertheless allow us to gain some insight into the relationship between language and thought as well as a certain perspective on the cultural basis of our own thought and the limitations of our own preconceptions.

The Sources

The texts that I take as my sources in this work were compiled in the period from the fifth to late third centuries B.C. I will include both Confucian and Daoist texts, with occasional reference to texts of other philosophical schools. This period was the golden age of Chinese philosophy, equivalent to the Axial age of Greek civilization. Politically, however, it was a period of increasingly vicious civil war in which numerous small states were defeated and taken over by their more powerful neighbors as "one hundred schools of thought" contended for intellectual dominance. The Zhou Dynasty (ca. 1100–222 B.C.) had been founded by an alliance of tribes. The Zhou empire may never have been quite as vast as that of the previous dynasty, the Shang (ca. 1700–1100 B.C.), but it covered much of the territory now designated as China, and the Zhou rulers created a type of feudal system in which their relatives and allies had control of various states.

In 771 B.C., rebellions and tribal incursions from the West forced the Zhou rulers to move their capital eastward. From this time on, their power began to decline and that of the individual states to increase. The period from 722–481 B.C. is known as the Spring and Autumn Period, after the title of a history of the state of Lu, attributed to Confucius (551–479 B.C.). In the following period, Zhou suzerainty ceased to even be acknowledged. Finally, in 221 B.C., the empire was unified under the rule of the First Emperor of Qin. Our texts were mainly compiled during this transitional period of intellectual as well a military ferment, known as the Warring States Period.

The Confucianists and the Daoists were only two of the many "schools of thought" that contended for influence during the fifth to third centuries B.C., but they were the two most enduring. Conceptually opposed to one another (and not entirely unitary as schools), they came to be regarded as two complementary aspects of human life in the later Chinese tradition: the public versus the private; or the conformist and intellectual as opposed to the natural and spontaneous . The Confucianists, whose major works were the *Analects* of Confucius, the *Mencius*, and the *Xunzi*, provided the political and ethical foundations for the Chinese state and society until modern times; the Daoists, whose major works were the *Laozi Daodejing* [*Lao-tzu Tao-te-ching*] and the *Zhuangzi* [*Chuang-tzu*], its creative and aesthetic impetus.

These are the primary texts that we shall consider herein. If my hypothesis that water and plant growth are a root metaphor of the Chinese conceptual scheme is correct, then the imagery discussed herein should be reflected in a vast range of philosophical, literary, and aesthetic expression, any of which could have been used to make the same point. Rather than attempting a broad survey, however, I will focus narrowly on those seminal Daoist and Confucian texts that formulated the language and served to set the terms of philosophical debate thereafter. I will also refer to other philosophical texts and schools, for example the *Mozi* (fourth century B.C.), and to texts and inscriptions of other periods, but only where they have a particular relevance.

The earliest text under consideration is the *Analects* (*Lunyu* 論語) of Confucius (551–479 B.C.). Confucius was the first philosopher in ancient China; that is, he was the first thinker to form a school of followers who recorded his thoughts and transmitted them to posterity in the form of a text. This text—known in English as the *Analects*—contains mainly short statements, often only one or two sentences long. These are not actually "sayings," but particular remarks of Confucius recorded by his disciples or their followers. They depend on extensive commentaries and the later tradition for their full import, but the importance of this text cannot be exaggerated. The *Analects* were the touchstone for all later philosophical writing. They provided much of the terminology and established the major concerns of philosophical discussion. That the Daoist Zhuangzi chose to put many of his own philosophical meditations into the mouth of Confucius, claiming Confucius' authority for his own opinions, is one indicator of Confucius' paramount importance even in ancient times. Ironic as this device may have been—Confucius is consistently made to recognize the superiority of Daoist positions—it does demonstrate Confucius' primacy. Similarly, the followers of Laozi felt that claiming Laozi was a teacher of Confucius was in their interest.

Mencius—or Mengzi 孟子 as he is known in Chinese—was a follower of Confucius who lived in the fourth century B.C. The text, which bears his name and contains mainly records of his conversations, was compiled soon after his death. We may surmise that the terse statements in the *Analects* served as the basis for an oral commentary when the teachings were passed down from teacher to student. Although the *Mencius* would also have been taught with an oral commentary, the text is fuller and it contains a more coherently expressed philosophical system. Thus, the *Mencius* was at least as influential historically as the *Analects* and Confucianism is known as much through this text as through that of its founder. Indeed, the *Mencius* and the *Laozi Daodejing* are probably the two most influential of all Chinese texts throughout history.

Traditionally—and apocryphally—Laozi was said to be an older contemporary of Confucius who advised him about ritual matters. The authorship and date of the *Laozi* are open to debate, but I take the text as roughly contemporaneous with the *Mencius*. On the one hand, as D. C. Lau has pointed out, Mencius takes care to oppose rival philosophical schools, but does not mention the *Laozi*. This suggests that the text was not known to him—or at least that he did not consider it significant as a contender in the battle for political influence. On the other, as Lau has also observed, many of the ideas in the *Laozi* are associated with a number of thinkers of the late fourth to early third century B.C. The contents of the *Laozi* are probably not entirely coherent in their origin or date, but the text in its present form, by and large, makes sense as a product of this golden age in the development of early Chinese philosophical thought.[4] Some scholars date this text even later but the recent discovery of a fragmentary (and as yet unpublished) *Laozi* written on bamboo slips in a middle Warring States tomb are conclusive evidence that some form of the text was in existence before the Han.

In 1973, archaeologists unearthed two copies of this text written on silk from a Han Dynasty (206 B.C.–A.D. 220) tomb, at Mawangdui, near Changsha, in Hunan Province. An inventory slip (to record the grave goods buried with the deceased) tells us that the burial took place on the equivalent of 4 April, 168 B.C. People were forbidden to write the characters in the names of deceased emperors and these tabooed characters are one means of dating a text. Of the two manuscripts from Mawangdui, Copy A observed no Han Dynasty taboos at all and so we may surmise that it was copied down before the death of the first Han emperor in 195 B.C. Copy B observed the taboos on the founder's name, but not those of his successor and so it must have been copied between 195 and 180 B.C. The two manuscripts are not identical, but they are very close and most scholars regard them as representatives of a single textual tradition. Reference to the *Laozi* in the following work will generally refer to a collation of these two manuscripts, although I will also refer to the transmitted versions of the text.[5] Since this is not a study of the development of ideas but an attempt to demonstrate an underlying conceptual scheme in early philosophical thought, I will "lump" rather than "split" when it comes to the dating of texts.

The *Analects* of Confucius and the *Laozi*, for example, might be split into chronological layers, but for the purpose of this study, I regard them both as cohesive texts.

Traditionally, the *Zhuangzi* and the *Laozi* have been grouped together as the two major texts of Daoist thought. The *Zhuangzi* is traditionally divided into three sections, the Inner Chapters, the Outer Chapters, and Mixed Chapters. I will primarily be concerned with the Inner Chapters, that is, those which most scholarly opinion attributes to Zhuangzi or Zhuang Zhou, who lived from middle of the fourth century into the early third century B.C. The scholarly debate about the relative dating of the *Laozi* and *Zhuangzi* is not easily resolved. On the one hand, we will find that the Inner Chapters of the *Zhuangzi* present another vision based on the same metaphoric roots as the *Laozi* and share some of the same terminology. On the other hand, few—if any— of these passages appear to have a direct derivation from the *Laozi*, in contrast to passages from the later sections.

The Outer and Mixed Chapters include much heterogeneous material, some of which may be as late as the very end of the third century. Although my primary concern is with the Inner Chapters, the later sections of the *Zhuangzi* are sometimes useful as examples which extend the range of imagery. In the later sections, particularly those that A. C. Graham has labeled "syncretic," we also find examples of more complex and sophisticated use of the terminology under consideration. Although I will make some reference to this, detailed analysis is beyond the purview of the present study.

Xunzi (310–219 B.C.) represents another branch of the Confucian school and he is not only later than Mencius—with whom he disputes certain issues—the text is also influenced by certain Daoist ideas.[6] This is the latest text that will be included in our corpus. In this text, we find more conscious and abstract systems have begun to develop. Technical terminology is used in a much more self-conscious and deliberate manner, as it is in the later sections of the *Zhuangzi*. For example, in the *Xunzi,* the reason that a gentleman gazes at a great river is given an elaborate and systematic explanation. Since my primary interest is in the initial conceptualization based on root metaphor rather than the development of the concepts, I will use the *Xunzi* in a limited manner only.

Root Metaphors and Conceptual Schemes

In *Metaphors We Live By,* George Lakoff and Mark Johnson argued that we think in metaphor, that our perception of reality in our everyday thinking is based on the concrete imagery of metaphoric structures. By using metaphor and mental imagery we are able to think imaginatively as well as abstractly. These structures are reflected in our literal language. On the abstract level, "so-called intellectual concepts, for example, the concepts in a scientific theory, are often—perhaps always—based on metaphors that have a physical and/or cultural basis. . . . The intuitive appeal of a scientific theory has to do with how well its metaphors fit one's experience." Thus, "the most fundamental values in a culture will be coherent with the metaphoric structure of the most fundamental concepts in the culture."[7]

Let us take as an example, time. I do so in part because time seems to be Lakoff and Johnson's most frequent example in their effort to demonstrate the way we think metaphorically on an everyday basis. Moreover, I will discuss time again in the course of this work with relation both to the metaphor of the stream of water and that of plant life. The manner in which the ancient Chinese conceived of time radically differentiates their conceptual scheme from our own. A full treatment of ancient Chinese ideas of time would require at least another book, so the following comments are only a brief illustration of what I mean by metaphoric thinking.

Time is an intellectual concept that requires a metaphoric model; that is, since time has no concrete reality, we need some sort of imagery or model in order to conceptualize it. Thus, the manner in which we think about time is a consequence of the metaphor on which we base our thinking. On an everyday basis in the modern world, as Lakoff and Johnson point out, we tend to think of time as a limited resource or commodity. Even those of us who would only use the saying Time Is Money in a jocular manner speak—and conceive—of time as something that we can save or spend; invest, budget, borrow, share or spare; win or lose. We even act accordingly. The root metaphors used to conceptualize time are of fundamental importance in the distinction between the Chinese and European systems of thought. Historically, in the West, various metaphoric models have been used to describe time scientifically as an intellectual concept. Newton, for example, used the analogy of a geometrical straight line. In this model, moments of absolute time were understood as analogous to the continuous sequence of points on the line.[8] Such a model is also associated with a progressive idea of history in which time moves forward without repeating itself.

In the Judeo-Christian tradition, the mortal world was created by God at a particular time and it will come to an end one day. In this scheme, two types of time are contrasted: there is the unending, eternal time of God as opposed to the bounded time of the mortal world. Following the Christian tradition, we count time from a single date, the birth of Christ (mythically, a new beginning of the world and thus a reenactment of the creation story) and, potentially at least, there is a final date, that of the apocalypse. We also conceive of the lives of individuals as discrete units, with a beginning (birth) and an end (death), during which each person is morally responsible for their own acts before the God who made them and to whom they must answer at the end of this time span.

There is no Classical Chinese word equivalent in meaning to the English word *time*. In the *Analects* (IX.17), we are told that Confucius, standing by a river, said, "What passes is perhaps like this: day and night it never lets up." In this passage, the imagery of the river suggests time passing, just as it did for his contemporary Heraclitus when he said that you cannot step into the same river twice. However, a specific term for "what passes" or "passes by"—what we call *time*—is noticeably absent.[9] Nevertheless, a Chinese word, sometimes translated as "time," *shi* 時, is a key term in early Chinese philosophy. The original meaning of *shi* is "season." By extension, it also means seasonality or timeliness and refers to doing something at the appropriate time, the time or season at which an action can succeed. *Shi* is meaningful in the context of a natural order to which people, as other living things including plants, must correspond in their actions if they are to flourish and achieve success in life. However, it is not equivalent to our idea of "time" and it cannot be used to discuss the phenomenon of time passing for which Confucius used the metaphor of a river.

Just as there is no Classical Chinese word equivalent to the English *time*, there is no English word that may be readily used to translate the Chinese *shi*. In early Chinese texts, there is no story of *abnihilo* creation, no story of an event like the creation story in Genesis which describes the creation of the world out of nothing and marks the beginning of time.[10] In Chinese chronologies, time is not counted from a single date, like the birth of Christ, but again and again from repeated historical beginnings— from the foundation of a dynasty, or the assumption of a royal reign within that dynasty. On the personal level, individual lives are, of course, bounded by birth and death, but the life of each person is also regarded as a link within the continuum of the ancestral lineage.

This distinction may be attributed to contrasting metaphoric structures: the biblical creation story takes the dramatic event of animal birth as its metaphor; the Chinese ancestral lineage, the continuum of plant reproduction. On the one hand, in our conceptual scheme, humans are readily classified together with animals, but a radical distinction is made between animals and plants. In Chinese, on the other hand, humans, animals, and plants are habitually classified together (as *wu* 物, "living things"), so that the pattern of reproduction which is shared by both plants and animals, including humans, is more readily apparent.

Sinologists are in the habit of describing Chinese ideas of time as cyclical, that is, Chinese time goes in circles rather than straight lines. But the idea of a "cycle" derives from a play on our own geometrical metaphor for time, as does the alternative, sometimes suggested, of a spiral. The use of the term *cycle* emphasizes repeating patterns as opposed to linear ideas of progress. Thus, it is helpful as a means of differentiating the Chinese concept from the Western metaphor of a straight line. It is not, however, a Chinese metaphor for describing time. As we shall see in the following, both water and plants provide metaphoric roots of early Chinese ideas about time. Water, in the form of the stream with a natural spring as its source, provides a model for ideas of both transience and continuity. Plants, with their annual patterns of change, for the concept of *shi* 時, and, in their reproductive continuum, for the concept of lineage.

Philosophy requires the formulation of terminology, an abstact language in which to theorize. This language is inevitably based on concrete imagery. What Lakoff and Johnson call the "metaphoric structure of the most fundamental concepts in a culture" is what I call "root metaphor." The use of the word *metaphor* in this context may be somewhat confusing. I am not concerned here with metaphor in the usual sense of figural language or with the use of concrete imagery to restructure abstract ideas, but with the concrete roots of the earliest abstractions. In other words, the 'root metaphor' is a concrete model that is inherent in the conceptualization of the "abstract" idea. The abstract idea derives from the process of analogy, rather than the analogy illustrating the idea.

The distinction that I wish to make here can be seen with reference to an important antecedent to this work in which Donald Munro observed that the most important metaphors used by the Song Dynasty (A.D. 960–1279) neo-Confucian philosopher Zhu Xi were water, plants and the family network. Munro states, for example, with regard to his use of plant metaphor, "[Zhu Xi's] theory is that principle/humaneness/human nature is the immaterial structure . . . from which all behavioral forms of love actualize. Thus, humaneness is the root, and brotherly love the sprouts, or principle is the root and love is the sprout, not vice versa. To structure the mind by means of the plant analogy is to say that the mind's major active traits are vitality and affection. . . ."[11]

Although Munro recognized that this metaphor can be traced back to the *Analects*, in his discussion of Zhu Xi's philosophy he nevertheless assumed that the plant was a literary metaphor by means of which Zhu Xi structured preexisting abstract concepts. My argument is that Chinese concepts of the mind and human nature were structured from the very beginning by an analogy

13

with the growth of plants. By Zhu Xi's time, the concepts had undergone many centuries of independent development as abstract ideas, and Zhu Xi undoubtedly thought of them as abstractions. In making his metaphors, he probably thought he was rediscovering the core of Confucianism and, indeed, when he rediscovered their metaphoric roots, he was.

My concern is thus with the models which underlay early Chinese conceptual thinking. My argument is not that water and plant life were literary metaphors, metaphors in the conventional sense of concrete images used to illustrate and structure philosophical concepts, but that they provided the *root metaphors* of many of the primary philosophical concepts. Such root metaphors are one aspect of what philosophers often call *conceptual schemes*. Many philosophers have understood these as logical propositions. A. C. Graham, however, argued that they should be defined in terms of patterns of names and categories that are prior to the formulation of any propositions.[12]

As Graham has stated, "at the root of the systems of propositions called 'conceptual schemes' by philosophers, there are patterns of perception which are pre-logical. . . . That all thinking is grounded in analogization shows up especially clearly when we try to come to grips with the thought of another civilisation."[13] These names and categories are spontaneously correlated to express meaning in patterns that reflect their metaphoric structures and are particular to their conceptual scheme. The significance of different patterns of names and categories becomes evident as soon as we try to translate one language into another, especially when those languages have no genetic relationship to one another.

Anyone who has attempted to translate Classical Chinese texts into a Western language will be aware that the terms used in the Chinese texts represent different categories of meaning than those of the language into which they are translated. Translation inevitably sets up networks of relationships and resonances that are quite different from those of the original language. For example, two terms that I will discuss at length in the course of this work, *xing* 性 and *ziran* 自然, are both commonly translated into English as "nature," but the two terms have no semantic relationship to one another in Chinese and the Chinese terms are quite different in meaning.

The translation "nature" for these two Chinese words not only sets up relationships between them that are not a part of the original conceptual scheme; it also has implications from our own conceptual scheme of a transcendent reality that was nonexistent in ancient China. These implications are present, for example, in such English terms as *laws of nature, mother nature*, and so on. In ancient China, there was a concept of an order which we may call natural. Furthermore, the earth is spoken of as a mother in a dual relationship with the sky or heaven (*tian* 天), which played the role of "father." In some contexts, the sky/heaven which governed the seasons may also appropriately be translated as nature. However, there was no concept of "nature" as a distinct entity that might prescribe—or act in accordance with—"law" or that might be called "mother."

Logical propositions depend on patterns of names and categories for their meaning and these are different in different languages. One can convey the central thrust of words and sentences—their *focal meaning* as it is sometimes called—in translation. However, the meaning of translated words and sentences merely overlaps with the meaning in the original language. Because some of the implications of the original are always left out in translation and new possibilities are inevitably suggested, translation cannot duplicate meaning precisely. When languages—and the conceptual schemes within which they operate—have no common historical origins, the distance between the meaning of the original and the translation is inevitably greater.

Since two sentences in two different languages are never exactly the same in meaning, one cannot, as Graham observed, logically negate a proposition made in one language in any other language. For example, we may translate "Grass is green" into Classical Chinese as "*Cao qing ye* 草青也." However, *cao* has a broader sense than grass, including straw, wild plants, and herbs. *Qing* is the color of grass and other living plants, but it includes gray and shades of blue and black. Indeed, its range of color is precisely that which cognitive anthropologists have distinguished as the "dark-cool-wet" color as opposed to "light-warm-dry"—

red, yellow, and white—in color systems that distinguish only two categories, even though the Chinese already had a more complex system when *qing* first appeared as a color in the Zhou Dynasty. Green, however, is one of the eleven basic color categories based on intensity, all of which are used in English.[14]

The grammar of the Chinese sentence also implies a different type of logical relationship.[15] The verb "to be" in English, as in many related languages, has both an existential sense and a grammatical usage as a copula. This conjunction of usages has had important implications in the history of Western philosophy. Classical Chinese, however, has no verb that is equivalent to either English usage. Where English uses the copula *is* (A is B), Classical Chinese uses the final particle *ye* (A B *ye*), but the logical relationship between A and B is not quite the same as in the Chinese. A B *ye* means that A belongs to the category B. If we were to translate *cao qing ye* back into English, a more literal translation would be: "As for grass, it belongs to the category of green."

The negative in Chinese is made by the addition of another grammatical particle, *fei* 非: *cao fei qing ye* (*ye* may be omitted in negative statements). Graham's point was that the acceptance of the idea of a conceptual scheme is not an acceptance of the idea of the relativity of truth because the truth of any statement can only be affirmed or denied in the language in which it is made. That the English proposition "Grass is green" is true, does not necessarily mean that the Chinese translation *cao qing ye* is so. Furthermore, although the logical proposition "grass is green" is negated in English as "grass is not green," grass not being green would not preclude *cao* from being *qing*, nor would the Chinese negative *Cao fei qing* 草非青 preclude the possibility that the grass is green. In other words, different conceptual schemes yield different insights and their truth can logically only be affirmed or denied in their own terms.

Moreover, no language is an isolated system; each has its own particular history, which is cultural as well as linguistic. Thus, the pattern of names and categories which characterize any particular language and conceptual scheme is not arbitrary, but historically and culturally derived. Because conceptual terms are grounded in analogization, they are interrelated in a complex manner that reflects their metaphoric structure. These interrelationships include not only patterns of correlation and opposition, such as those with which Graham was concerned, but a more complex set of dynamic relationships. For example, concepts that are modeled on water in its various forms have inherent structural relationships which remain even at the level of abstraction, but cannot be conveyed in translation.

We need not accept all of Lakoff and Johnson's ideas about thinking in metaphor to recognize that the formulation of the earliest intellectual concepts in the formative period of a philosophical discourse, be it East or West, will draw on the root metaphors of that civilization. Root metaphors often derive from the mythical narratives of a religious tradition. For example, the importance of a creation myth to the ontology of Western philosophy has often been noted. Roger Ames, for example, has argued that "the notion of initial beginning, whether it pertains to the cosmos as a whole or to the creatures that populate it, must surely have a significant, if not determinative influence over the way a culture comes to conceive of the nature and order of things."[16] In contrast to this idea of an initial beginning, Tu Weiming and others have stressed the idea of continuity of being as a basic motif of Chinese ontology with far-reaching implications.[17]

In recent years, comparative philosophers and sinologists have become increasingly aware of the importance of divesting our interpretations of Chinese philosophy of our own preconceptions. As Frederick Mote has stated, "History, culture, and people's conceptions of their ideal roles all must be explained in terms of Chinese cosmology, and not—if we really want to understand Chinese civilization—by implicit analogy to ours. . . . Hence, the records of Chinese culture must be interpreted, and the texts translated and retranslated until our inadvertent uses of historical and cultural analogy are detected, weighed, and, if necessary, corrected."[18] We cannot, however, divest our interpretations of Chinese culture of our own cultural analogies simply by translating and retranslating the texts. Nor can we do so by "comparative philosophy," which uses the more abstract—but no less culturally biased—specialist language of the professional philosopher.

17

We must begin by exposing the metaphors that underlie the Chinese terminology and imbue it with meaning. Indeed, we *cannot* divest our interpretations of Chinese thought of implicit analogies from our own conceptual scheme *until* we recognize the root metaphors of Chinese thought. We can, of course, never entirely comprehend another conceptual scheme, and our ability to divest ourselves of preconceptions is further diminished when we use the medium of our own language to translate and interpret another system of thought. Nevertheless, by recognizing the root metaphors of Chinese thought, we can at least begin to understand the Chinese terminology more accurately and this should enable us to interpret the texts and the philosophy that they express more clearly.

The structure of early Chinese religion is fundamentally different from the Greek, Judeo-Christian, and other Indo-European religions. Thus, a few comments about the nature of early Chinese religion may be useful to orient the reader before turning to the subject at hand.

Early Chinese Religion

I have already referred to the close relationship of the Western religious traditions and the ontology of Western philosophy. There is no religious narrative, such as the Bible, in the Chinese tradition and what we know about early Chinese religion is primarily from records of ritual practices. These include divination inscriptions on shell and bone, the so-called oracle bone inscriptions, made by the last kings of the Shang Dynasty (ca. 1700–1100 B.C.), and inscriptions on bronze vessels from the Western Zhou Dynasty (ca. 1100–772 B.C.). A full review of the relationship of the early Chinese religious tradition and the ontology of Chinese philosophy is beyond the scope of this work. However, certain aspects of early Chinese religion are particularly relevant to our understanding of why Chinese philosophers assumed that common principles govern the human and natural worlds. I will review these aspects very briefly below. They include: (1) the ritual structure of Chinese ancestor worship in which the individual was part of a lineage that included both the living and the dead; (2) the worship of nature spirits together with the ancestors; and (3) the role of *tian* 天, "sky/heaven," as a supreme force with power over the natural and human worlds.

From the point of view of the individual, the central rites of Chinese religion from at least Neolithic times onward were food offerings given to the ancestors in exchange for benevolence or at least to prevent their malevolence. Our earliest written evidence for Chinese ritual practice is from the divinations inscribed on bone and shell made by the kings of the Shang Dynasty. From these inscriptions, which are primarily concerned with making offerings to the spirits and thus avoiding their curses, we can deduce an outline of Shang religious structure.

The most common topic for divination by the Shang kings was the appropriate food offerings to be made to an ancestor. An assumption underlying the offerings to the ancestors and the divinations made about them was that people continued to need food after death. The spirits of the dead also continued to exercise power over their descendants who had the duty of providing them with nurture. Thus, another common topic for divination by the Shang kings was the possibility that the royal ancestors would visit some calamity on them or their people. The most common calamities were natural disasters, such as drought and crop failure, but human illness and defeat in warfare were other possibilities.

Within this ritual system, the role of the individual was as a member of his ancestral lineage. The ritual of food offerings to the ancestors served to connect the living with the dead. As I have already discussed at some length elsewhere, a consequence of this structure is that there is no "other world" of supernatural beings which is comparable to but radically different than the mundane one.[19] The ancestral spirits related directly to the living through the ritual of food offerings. They did not have a life after death in which they fraternized with one another. They were not gods like those of ancient Greece who lived on Mount Olympus, eating ambrosia and drinking nectar, occasionally dallying with humans but mainly concerned with one another. Nor were they souls who stood before an almighty god who created them and to whom they were answerable.

The Chinese spirits were simply human beings, dead ones, who continued to require nurture and to exercise power over their descendants, but they made no moral demands and did not exercise any moral sanctions according to some higher, transcendental law. The ritual structure of Chinese ancestor worship is, however, one key to understanding the ontology of morality in the Chinese conceptual scheme. Such concepts as *xiao* 孝, "filial piety" and *li* 禮, "rites" or "ceremony," for example, which are the central tenets for behavior in Confucianism derived directly from this religious background. Although I will not analyze this relationship herein, we shall see in the following that the individual within the ancestral lineage was conceptualized in terms of plant imagery in which the individual was part of a continuous pattern of generation, reproduction, decline, and death.

At the top of this structure was *Shang Di* 上帝, the "lord on high." The term *di* was also used for the Shang ancestors in the main line of descent. This suggests that he too was the spirit of a dead person or at least that he had certain human characteristics. However, Shang Di was such a shadowy figure that some scholars have even suggested that the term was a collective one for a group of ancestral spirits.[20] Since Shang Di in the later Chinese tradition was always correlated with a single king who ruled "all under the sky/heaven," I think it more likely that the "lord on high" of the Shang was also singular. Nevertheless, he was simply a power, not a personality. Most important, he controlled the weather, "ordering" the rain and clouds and "sending down" drought.

Within this structure, there is no clear differentiation between the human and natural worlds. Shang Di exercised power over both. Furthermore, the power of the most distant ancestors— and the sacrifices that they received—are similar to those of the nature spirits. These were the spirits of certain natural phenomenon, primarily rivers, mountains, and earth. We know very little about how the Shang conceived of the nature spirits, but the names of the rituals that they performed to them and the offerings made in the course of these rituals were the same ones that were given to the high ancestors. Furthermore, the powers of the high ancestors and nature spirits were similar; the primary powers of both types of spirits were to curse the weather and affect the harvest by causing drought or rain.

When the Zhou overthrew the Shang, they identified *tian* 天, the sky/heaven, with Shang Di. *Tian* means "sky" but in its role as the supreme force, it is conventionally translated as "heaven," giving it religious overtones from our own tradition in which heaven is either a place in the sky where the souls of the good go after death or a euphemism for God. This sounds more natural in English—the translation of "sky" for the supreme power is unsettlingly graphic to the English reader. To say that the ruler of China, especially in the sophisticated imperial court of later times, was the "son of the sky" sounds very strange to us. However, the role of "heaven" in English as a euphemism for God gives *tian* a specifically anthropomorphic character and suggests a supreme creator in a manner which obscures the meaning of the Chinese term. This equation is compounded when Shang Di is translated as *God*.

Although *tian* was identified with Shang Di, the "high lord" of the Shang people, at the beginning of the Zhou Dynasty, it was also, quite literally, the sky. In nature, *tian* governed the seasons. And with regard to people, it also determined the appropriate "times" at which a dynasty might be changed, that is, when one lineage might be exchanged for another in its dominance over the world "below the sky" or, as convention has it, "under heaven." The two roles are never distinguished and this may provide the key to the assumption in the philosophical tradition that people could determine principles which are applicable to the human world by studying plants, water, and other natural phenomena.

If *tian* was originally a nature spirit rather than a high god, like those of the mountains and rivers in the Shang oracle bone inscriptions, its supremacy would then derive from the importance of the sky in a natural hierarchy. The physical import of *tian* as the "sky" is readily evident when it is paired with *di* 地, "earth." This pairing is common to both the Confucian and the Daoist texts. Furthermore, in the Daoist texts, in which the *dao* or "way" supplants *tian* as a first principle, *tian* and *di* are sometimes described as a male/female pair responsible for the generation of all living things: humans, plants and animals.[21] This suggests that the literal identification of *tian* as "sky" was always an essential aspect of its identity.

I have referred already to the concept of *shi* 時 in ancient China. It had a basic meaning of season which was extended to mean the appropriate time at which something can succeed, that is, seasonality or timeliness. *Tian* 天 controlled the *shi* of the natural world—presumably because seasonal changes were measured by observing the movements of the heavenly bodies—the suns, moons, stars, and constellations—in the sky. *Tian* also served to determine the appropriate times at which something could succeed in the human world, as in the world of nature. Thus, *tian*, the "sky/heaven," was responsible for the rise and fall of the dynasties on the assumption that the moral order of human society, like that of the natural world, has a definite temporal pattern. As we shall see in the following, *tian* remained the supreme principle in the Confucian texts, but it was replaced in this role by *dao* in the Daoist tradition.

The role of sky/heaven as both a natural force and power over the human world provides a key to understanding the assumption made by the Chinese philosophers that one could derive principles applicable to the human world from the study of natural phenomenon such as water and plants. Although both the Indo-European religious traditions and Western philosophy depend on the assumption of transcendence, an idea of an unchanging reality, be it a deity or natural laws, in contrast to the changing world of man, the structure of Chinese religion was such that the ancestral lineage tied the world of the spirits directly to that of the living. There was thus a continuum between this world and that of the spirits, rather than a sphere of transcendent reality that stands in radical contrast to the mundane one. Furthermore, at least in early times, there was no particular ritual distinction between the ancestral spirits and those of natural phenomenon. Thus the Chinese worldview was a holistic one.

Water and Plant Life

If one assumes that common principles govern the natural world and the human mind, then ethical values can be discussed by reference to natural principles. The fondness of Chinese philosophers for analogy as a means of argumentation is well known. The use of analogy is often dismissed as a rhetorical device. However, once we recognize this assumption that common principles governed the natural and human worlds, then we can see that argument by analogy—the primary method of argumentation in ancient China—had a more serious purpose. It was used and achieved its validity because of the assumption of a real parallel.

The passage with which we began, in which Confucius praised water, is not an isolated one. Confucius' interest in water as a means of understanding the principles of human behavior is well-attested. According to the *Analects,* Confucius, "standing by a river, said, 'What passes is perhaps like this. Day and night it never lets up'" (IX.17).[22] Another passage from the *Analects* tells us that Confucius said, "the intelligent find joy in water"; whereas "the humane find joy in mountains. The intelligent are lively; the humane, still. The intelligent are happy; the humane, long-lived"(VI.22). Moreover, according to a further passage from the *Mencius,* Confucius urged his disciples to take notice of the wisdom inherent in the nursery rhyme, "The water of the Cang Lang River is clear, so we may wash our capstrings; the water of the Cang Lang River is dirty, so we may wash our feet," observing that water "takes the principle upon itself (*zi qu zhi* 自取之), just as men invite insult upon themselves" (IVA.8). According to Mencius, "There is an art to looking at water (*guan shui you shu* 觀水有術)" (VIIA.24).

The tradition that water was a source of knowledge for Confucius is continued in the *Xunzi* where we are told that Zi Gong inquired of Confucius who was watching a river flowing east, "Why is it that when a gentleman sees a great river, he always gazes at it?" And Confucius replied:

Water, which extends everywhere and gives everything life without acting (*wuwei* 無爲) is like virtue (*de* 德). Its stream, which descends downward, twisting and turning but always following the same principle, is like rightness (*yi* 義). Its bubbling up, never running dry, is like the way (*dao* 道). Where there is a channel to direct it, its noise is like an echoing cry and its fearless advance into a hundred meter valley, like valor (*yong* 勇). Used as a level, it is always even, like law (*fa* 法). Full, it does not require a ladle, like correctness (*zheng* 正). Compliant and exploratory, it reaches to the tiniest point, like perceptiveness (*cha* 察). That which goes to it and enters into it, is cleansed and purified, like the transformation of goodness (*shanhua* 善化). In twisting around ten thousand times but always going eastward, it is like will (*zhi* 志). That is the reason that when a gentleman sees a great river, he will always look upon it. (28 *You Zuo*, pp. 390–1)[23]

In sum, a gentleman studies water because all of the principles to which he aspires are embodied in its many manifestations.

This equation between water and the principles of human conduct depends on an assumption that the same principles govern the natural and human worlds for its legitimacy. Thus, Confucius meditated upon water; and the Confucian Xunzi later attempted to systematize the relationship between water's various forms and people's moral qualities. This assumption of a correspondence between the principles which inform both water and human conduct was not limited to the Confucians; it was generally assumed in all early philosophical texts. Nor was the imagery the provenance of any particular school. For example, water which moves forward without force, giving life to everything, is described in the *Xunzi* as *wuwei* 無爲, "without action" or "doing nothing," a term that is particularly associated with Daoism.[24]

The same image of water extending everywhere and giving everything life without taking deliberate action, is apparent in the *Laozi* (Dao 8) which states, "The highest good is like water. Water's goodness is that it benefits the myriad living things, yet does not contend and dwells in places which the multitude detest. Thus, it approximates the Way."[25] Water, which is here equated with the *dao* and proclaimed the highest good, is also important in the *Zhuangzi* and furthermore in the *Mozi, Hanfeizi,* and all early Chinese philosophical writing. Although this study is confined to philosophical thought from the fifth to third centuries B.C., the imagery pervades later Chinese philosophy and aesthetic creation.

In reading early Chinese philosophical texts, we should, I believe, take them at their word: Confucius did study water and Laozi used it as a model for his concept of the Way. Because the philosophers assumed that the same cosmological principles underlie human behavior, they sought to derive principles about the natural world by studying water and natural phenomena which would enable them to understand man and his place in the natural order. This assumption was implied when they came to formulate abstract philosophical concepts about the nature of the cosmos and it is inherent in their terminology. The imagery is thus intrinsic in the philosophical concepts and inseparable from them. This is evident not only in an analysis of particular concepts; it is also reflected in the dynamic relationships between the concepts.

Once formulated, the concepts developed as abstract ideas with other layers of meaning and connotations. Thus, there is no simple one to one relationship between concept and image. I will discuss the manner in which both water and plants provided models for particular philosophical ideas in the following chapters, but many concepts refer to more than a single metaphor, depending on the context and the precise meaning that is being expressed. For example, we will find a close association between the concept of *xin* 心, the "mind/heart" and water imagery when thinking and emotional states are in question, but an association with plant imagery when the issue is goodness. Furthermore, new metaphors and other imagery may be used to express ideas about preestablished concepts. In other words, the concepts were abstract ideas grounded in metaphor. The meaning and interrelationships of the concepts can be better understood with reference to that imagery, but once formulated they are abstract ideas, not a sort of picture language. Since they are ideas, they have a conceptual life of their own that is distinct from their origins. However, because the natural phenomena served as models in the formulation of the abstract philosophical principles, the imagery associated with these phenomena is still implicit in the vocabulary of philosophical discourse. Moreover, because the imagery is inherent in the vocabulary and concepts, the root metaphor continues to provide an implicit structure to the relationships between words and ideas.

Procedure

In order to avoid projecting an alien structure on the philosophical ideas, I will proceed from the concrete to the abstract, from imagery to philosophy—from language to idea. My intention in beginning with the concrete imagery is to reveal the inherent structure of the metaphoric system. I will first discuss water and then plants. In the following chapter, I will begin my exploration by asking "How did early Chinese philosophers think about water?" This is a literal question and it will be answered by analyzing the language with which the philosophers described water and what they had to say about it. In this chapter, I will use all of the texts mentioned above, including the later sections of the *Zhuangzi* and the *Xunzi*. Occasional reference will be made to other texts as well in order to establish the full range of water's cognitive potential in the early textual tradition.

Having analyzed the manner in which water was described in the texts, I will turn to key philosophical concepts which share the language and characteristics associated with water in Chapter 3. I will argue that water imagery is inherent in these concepts and that their meaning and interrelationships can be elucidated by reference to this imagery. The concepts under consideration will include *dao* 道, the "way," *wuwei* 無爲, "doing nothing," *xin* 心, the "mind/heart," and *qi* 氣 "breath" or "vital energy." My primary texts here and in the following chapter will be the *Analects* of Confucius, the *Mencius*, the *Xunzi*, the *Laozi*, and the *Zhuangzi*.

In Chapter 4, I will discuss the imagery associated with plants

26

and those concepts that can be elucidated with reference to the root metaphor of plant life. I will argue that a key difference between the Chinese and European conceptual schemes is the inclusion of plants, animals, and people within a single category of living things in China which served as a basis for theorization about the natural order. The concepts under discussion in this chapter will include *wu* 物, *xing* 性, *ren* 仁, *cai* 才, *duan* 端, *ziran* 自然, and *de* 德.

In Chapter 5, I will conclude by reviewing the manner in which the individual texts make use of the root metaphors of water and plant growth. I will pay particular attention to the *Mencius* and the *Laozi*, which I take as roughly contemporary, and which have especially coherent cosmologies. These cosmologies, as we shall see, in spite of their radically different philosophies, are based on an assumption that the same principles are found in the human and natural worlds and are grounded in the same root metaphor.

Although I have confined this study to a few core texts of the early Chinese philosophical tradition—those that were most influential in the development of all later Chinese thought—and will not attempt any broader analysis of the manner in which the concepts discussed herein developed in later times, readers acquainted with later Chinese philosophical and other literature will undoubtedly find the same themes recurring.

Chapter 2 ————————————

Water

Hence in a season of calm weather
Though inland far we be,
Our souls have sight of that immortal sea.
—William Wordsworth (1770–1850)

Although I draw my knife across the water, the river
continues to flow.
When I raise my cup to lessen my sorrows, the
sorrows only grow.
—Li Bai (701–762)

————————————

Figure 2. Fishing in the Clear Stream, anonymous, Sung Dynasty (960–1126). *National Palace Museum, Taipei, Taiwan, Republic of China.*

Water is a universal natural phenomenon, but we cannot assume that the ancient Chinese thought about water in the same manner that we do. Early Chinese texts do not praise the vast "immortal sea" which so lit the imagination of Wordsworth. When Confucius exclaimed "Water, ah water," he was not urging his followers to contemplate the infinite power of the almighty, but to meditate on the source of life which was before his very eyes. The water which most interested Chinese philosophers was that found in the great rivers and the small streams, and in the irrigation ditches which surrounded fields of grain. It was the rain and the pools which form from fallen rain, the ordinary rather than the infinite, that which sustains life and is experienced by all. From the contemplation of this most common and most variable of natural phenomena, the Chinese philosophers sought to understand the fundamental principles of life, principles that applied not only to the physical world, but also to human society. Thus, water served as a root metaphor in the formulation of abstract concepts that were the basis of a system of social and ethical values.

If water is a root metaphor of Chinese philosophy, then we must understand how the ancient Chinese thought about water in order to understand the implications of particular philosophical terms and how these terms are interrelated. Our first problem, then, is not the analysis of abstract ideas, but the concrete question of how the philosophers perceived water. How did early Chinese philosophers describe water? What language did they use and what were the attributes they assigned to it? What was the significance of these attributes? After investigating the meanings which the philosophers attached to water in its various forms in this chapter, we will then turn to the meaning of the philosophical concepts that share the language and characteristics associated with water. If my hypothesis is correct, then the meanings of particular conceptual terms will correspond to their metaphoric roots. Furthermore, the interrelationships between the terms should reflect the structure of the metaphor.

Shui 水, 'Water'

The Classical Chinese word conventionally translated as "water" is pronounced in modern Mandarin as *shui* (archaic pronunciation *hljuəj). The meaning of *shui* overlaps with that of the English word *water*, but is not identical. Thus, before analyzing how the philosophers describe water, we must look briefly at the meaning of the word itself. *Shui* 水 is a broader category than English "water." It connotes water as a substance, but it also refers to water as a natural phenomenon; that is, *shui* can mean "river," "flood," or "to flood," as well as "water" as such. Thus, for example, Confucius who gazed at a "river" *(shui)*, could also be said to gaze at "water" *(shui)*; and the intelligent one who found joy in "water" *(shui)*—as opposed to the humane man who finds joy in mountains—could also be said to find joy in "rivers" *(shui)* (see Ch. I, p. 23).

Rivers and floods are water, of course, and we should observe here, as elsewhere when we analyze Chinese words, that the system of categorization inherent in the Chinese language sets different boundaries from those of our own. Furthermore, even where categories overlap, their focus may be different. When we translate *shui* in any particular sentence into English, we are required to distinguish subcategories, such as "water," "river" or "flood" in the translation. We may recognize the relationship between these subcategories intellectually—that water, rivers, and floods are all aspects of the same natural phenomenon, but we nevertheless perceive them as semantically distinct. Thus, although the translation of any particular sentence is correct, that is, it correctly reflects the primary thrust of that particular sentence, the translation inevitably obscures the relationships between the categories inherent in the Chinese conceptual scheme and, at the literal level, between sentences. The categories in which we think and their interrelationships are thus determined by our language. In this sense, our thinking is inseparable from the language of our thought processes.

Although the Chinese writing system is not phonetic, Chinese characters are not simply ideographic as sometimes supposed. They represent words (or parts of words in the modern language), not objects or ideas; and they are made up of varying combinations of meaning and sound elements. This was true even in the earliest examples of the writing system now known, the oracle bone inscriptions of the second millennium B.C..[1] Nevertheless, we may reasonably assume that when a character was first created, the imagery chosen reflected contemporary ideas about the word it signified. And, just as the study of the Latin, Greek, or Anglo-Saxon roots of English words can help us to understand their history and the potential scope of their meaning, an analysis of the early forms of a Chinese character may reveal the history and semantic associations of the word for which it stands. Furthermore, the imagery contained in a written character continued to influence the manner in which people thought about a word in later times. This was true even though the imagery was sometimes misinterpreted by later writers who no longer understood its origin.

Although the writing system was already highly developed in the divination inscriptions of the Shang Dynasty (ca. 1700–1100 B.C.) commonly known as oracle bones, the imagery is more vivid and less stylized than in the later script. In modern script,[2] the character that represents *shui* is written: 水. The original character is a simple pictograph. Its earliest known forms are those found in the Shang oracle bone inscriptions where it was written as:

These are all closely related variants, the first of which is the antecedent of the modern forms of the character.

The character for *shui* depicts a stream or river. The long stroke (or strokes) denotes the bend of a river and this element is often used as a semantic element in river names, with or without the short lines. For example, the name of the river Huan (洹) was written as a combination of "water" (氵) and the phonetic element (亘), borrowed to represent the sound of the river's name. The variants in the oracle bone inscriptions include:

The short lines on the sides signify water in the form of drops or a stream.

Water is represented by a number of short strokes in many other characters. For example, a character that refers to ritual bathing, usually transcribed as 浴, was written as a man (亻) in a vessel (凵) with drops of water :

and the character for urination (尿) was written as a man from which a series of short strokes emanate:

In the oracle bone inscriptions of the Shang Dynasty, *shui* meant "flood" and "flooding," as well as "river," as it did in later texts. For example, divinations are often made to determine whether a calamity or curse should be "reported" to the ancestral spirits and *shui* "water" or "flooding" is one such calamity.

The earliest dictionary of Chinese characters is the *Shuowen Jiezi* 說文解字 (compiled at the end of the first century A.D.). Its title means "explaining writing and analyzing characters" and it attempts to explain the form of individual characters. The *Shuowen* dictionary explanations do not necessarily represent the historical origins of the characters accurately. There was a long history of development—over one thousand years—between this dictionary and the oracle bone inscriptions that are now the earliest extant forms of the characters but were unknown to the author of the *Shuowen*. However, the *Shuowen* explanations do represent scholarly understanding of the characters—and the words which the characters denote—in the Han Dynasty when the dictionary was compiled.

Although there had been some graphic development in the *Shuowen* character forms from those of the Shang Dynasty, the character, *shui*, was still written in a similar manner:

The *Shuowen* begins with a definition of the word: "Water *(shui)* is a standard *(zhun* 準*)."* *Zhun* is literally a carpenter's level and by extension, a moral standard. According to the *Zhuangzi*, for

34

example, the flat level surface of still water provided the model for the carpenter's level.[3]

The dictionary then goes on to describe the form of the character:

> "Its movement northward resembles the many rivers (*shui* 水) all flowing together."

In traditional Chinese cartography, north was at the bottom of the map rather than at the top. As the *Xunzi* has already told us (see p. 24), rivers in China flow east not north. So, the *Shuowen* reference is not to reality, but to the character *shui* with its downward pointing stream. The explanation also refers to five element theory in which water was correlated with north, wood with east, fire with south, metal with west, and earth with the center. This theory was well established by the first century A.D., but it was not yet current in the philosophical texts which are our main concern herein.

Let us now turn to the characteristics of water as described in the texts.

Water with a Source Flows Continuously

When the source of a river or stream is a spring, it is continually replenished. It wells up from the earth and flows ever forward. This is the attribute of water that Confucius admired in the passage from *Mencius* which I discussed briefly in the previous chapter (IVB.18). The following is my own translation, rather than that of D. C. Lau:

> Xuzi said: "Confucius frequently extolled water, saying, 'Ah water! Ah water!' What [principle] did he draw (*qu* 取) from water?"
> Mencius said: "The stream from a spring surges forth, not letting up day and night. It fills up the hollows and only then does it go forward to be released into the four seas. That which has a source is like this. What [Confucius] took

35

as a principle is simply this: in the seventh and eighth months, the rain collects and the irrigation ditches are all filled, but one can stand and wait for them to dry up. Therefore, a reputation which exceeds one's natural endowment is something of which a gentleman is ashamed."

In this passage, a stream that has a spring as its source (*yuan quan* 原泉) is contrasted with water that falls as rain from the sky. Rain, which has no source—or "root" (*ben* 本)—can fill the irrigation ditches and provide water for agriculture, but it quickly dries up, whereas water from a spring continues to flow. According to Mencius, Confucius drew the conclusion from the principle embodied by this natural phenomenon that reputation which does not have a person's natural endowment as a source for replenishment will not continue to flow, but dry up before one's very eyes, causing a gentleman to feel shame rather than honor.

The *Analects* of Confucius, compiled a century earlier than the *Mencius,* was more laconic, but the same expression "not letting up day or night" occurred in the passage:

"The master standing by a river, said, 'What passes (*shi zhe* ³u ªÌ) is perhaps like this. It does not let up day or night'." (IX.17)

Water with a source is something that continually replaces itself, an unending stream, like a reputation that may be passed down over the generations, or, more metaphysically, it is like "what passes," time itself.

The primary reference of *shi* 逝, which I have translated here as "pass" is to physical movement. The character is made up of a semantic element (辶), which signifies movement, and a phonetic element (折), indicating the pronunciation. It is defined in the early dictionaries as "going"[4] and often means to "go by" or "go past" or to "pass on" or "pass away," as water or things that float on water go past. For example, "Rocking gently, [the boat] passes by *(shi)*" (*Shijing* 44.2).[5] This line is from the *Book of Songs,* which was traditionally said to have been edited by Confucius and reached its final form at about the same time as the *Analects*. Similarly, *shi* is used in the *Mencius* (VA.2) to describe fish swimming away.

As we have already seen, there was no classical Chinese word equivalent to the English word 'time.' *Shi* 時[6] refers to the correct season, the right time, when something can successfully reach its fulfillment, or to timeliness in a natural order of repeating patterns of change, rather than to time as such. In the *Analects*, in the absence of a word that specifically means time passing, Confucius simply compares the passing stream with "passing away." What "passes" is both that which we call time and life itself.

In another passage from the *Analects*, *shi* 逝 is used explicitly with reference the passage of time: "The days and months pass by (*shi* 逝), but the harvest is not given to me" (XVII.1). In Classical Chinese, days and months were also literally "suns" and "moons" and so they could also be said to pass by in a literal sense. In later texts, *shi* 逝 is used as a conventional euphemism for death or dying, just as we speak of someone "passing away." For example, the *Han Shu* (first century A.D.) tells us of Sima Qian—the great historian who suffered the disgrace of castration in order to finish his history, "the ethereal (*hun* 魂) and corporeal (*po* 魄) souls are [things] which will take a long time to pass away (長逝); his personal resentment will have no extinction."[7] *Shi* is not, however, "passing on" which carries the implication of another world where one goes after death. Furthermore, as we can see from this passage, even the two souls in the Chinese tradition gradually pass away.

In the *Laozi*, *shi* is also one of the names that may be given to the nameless way, the *dao* 道:

> Not knowing its name, I call it the "way." If I am forced to give it a name, I say "great." "Great" is called "passing" (*shi* 時).[8] "Passing" is called "going far away." . . ." (*Dao* 25)

This passage, in which the way is associated with a river stream and encompasses the river's implication of time passing, will be discussed again in the following chapter.

Figure 3. Ten Thousand Riplets on the Yangzi, by Ma Yuan, Song Dynasty (960–1126). *Imperial Palace Museum, Beijing, China. Photograph Courtesy of Wenwu Press.*

Figure 4. The Yellow River Breaches its Course, by Ma Yuan, Song Dynasty (960–1126). *Imperial Palace Museum, Beijing, China. Photograph Courtesy of Wenwu Press.*

Water Flows along a Course

When water wells up from a spring, it does not flow haphazardly in any direction, but follows a course.

Early settlements were built by rivers and the water from these rivers was channeled into irrigation ditches. This was the basis of an agricultural society. The early philosophical texts tell us that the world was flooded with water in the time of Yao 堯, the first ruler named in these texts. The water rose so high it threatened the sky, but after several false starts, Yao appointed Yu 禹, who labored mightily, digging channels and building up mountains with the extra earth, so that the water flowed as rivers and streams within banks, finally emptying into the sea.[9]

This story of a great flood has a superficial similarity to the flood story of the Judeo-Christian tradition, but no Chinese account speaks of rain as the cause of the great flood and its cultural meaning is different. The role of this story in Chinese mythology is more closely equivalent to the biblical myth of the creation of the world than to that of Noah's flood which was sent down as a punishment to humankind by a transcendent God. Although the Chinese flood story does not mark the beginning of the world or the origin of mankind, the earliest forms of the Chinese story were part of a myth about giving order to the world and making it habitable for man. By directing the waters along river channels, the great Yu made settled agricultural life possible. The underworld in ancient China was water (the Yellow Springs). Quite possibly, this underworld was the source of the rising waters which flooded the world, as well as the ultimate source of all the rivers, but our texts are uninterested in what caused the flood and do not speculate about it. In this they are quite different from the Bible.

For the Chinese writers, the most important aspect of the flood was that the water did not have any channels to follow or else that it did not flow within them. Digging the river channels and directing the water so that it followed along them, flowing in an orderly manner was the first step toward creating a civilized world. This is the story, as told in the *Mencius*:

world was generated long ago; there is a time of order, and then a time of disorder. When it was the time of Yao, water flowed counter to its current (*ni xing* 逆行) and inundated the central states. Snakes and dragons lived in it. The people had nowhere to settle. Those in the low lands built nests and those on high, made cave dwellings. The *Documents* say, "The deluge is a warning to me." By "deluge," it means "water everywhere." [Yao] had Yu control it. Yu excavated the earth and channeled (*zhu* 注) it to the sea. He drove away the snakes and dragons, banishing them to the grassy marshland. The water moved along courses in the earth; these were the Jiang (Yangzi), Huai, He (Yellow River), and Han. The dangers and obstacles receded and the harm to people by birds and beasts diminished. Only then did people obtain level land to live on. (IIIB.9)

Yu's work here is described as bringing the unruly water under control by channeling it to the sea. Thus, people were able to live on the land.

In another closely connected passage, Mencius criticized a ruler who boasted of his irrigation works, comparing himself with the great Yu, by declaring that Yu, unlike the unfortunate ruler, used the "way of water" (*shui zhi dao* 水之道):

Yu's control over the water was [to make use of] the way of water. For this reason, Yu took the four seas as ravines. When water flows outside its courses, it is called a "deluge." A "deluge" is a flood. It is that which humane men detest. . . . (VIB.11)

By using the "way of water," Mencius meant that Yu took advantage of its natural tendency to flow downward and yield to obstacles. Because of this characteristic, water can easily be channeled. Thus, according to Mencius, Yu directed the water and controlled the flood by following water's natural inclination: "If knowledgeable men were like Yu in directing the water, then there would be no dislike of knowledge. Yu's means of directing water was to make the water move where it had no resistance (*xing qi suo wu shi* 行其所無事). If knowledgeable men would also make [people] move where there was no resistance, then their knowledge would be great indeed!" (IVB.26). In other words, Yu's success—like that of the knowledgeable or humane person—was in understanding that water follows the natural contours of the land, avoiding anything that might hinder its downward flow. A similar understanding by a ruler of what people like and dislike and the way in which they behave would result in a peaceful world.

In this passage, Mencius argued that the same principles that Yu used to control the flooding water can be used to rule the people. His description of water as having the natural tendency to avoid obstacles is similar to the frequent assertion in Daoist texts that water "avoids contending," which we shall discuss below. Furthermore, in the *Laozi*, the way itself (*dao* 道) is described as the "watercourse" or "irrigation channel" (*zhu* 注) "for the myriad living things (*wan wu* 萬物). It is the treasure of the good man and that by which the man who is not good can be preserved" (*De* 2; 62). *Zhu*, as a noun, is a channel for water—from which the myriad living things draw the water that gives them life—just as they draw metaphorically from the *dao*; as a verb, it can mean to draw water or make a channel for water, as we saw in Mencius' description of Yu's excavation of the riverbeds cited above. The relationship of the concept of *dao*, the "way" and a watercourse will be discussed in the following chapter.

Water Flows Downward

Water spontaneously moves downward. Indeed, it is this tendency of water to move downward that makes it possible to channel water and it is the reason that it will flow along a pre-established course or riverbed. That something which is not alive can move of its own accord was one of water's most fascinating characteristics to the ancient Chinese and the innate tendency of water to flow downward is one of its most important attributes in early Chinese philosophical thinking.

The recognition that water will always spontaneously move

. is the key to Mencius' victory in a famous passage in
.e debates human nature with a contemporary opponent,
.i. Mencius argued that human nature was good; Gaozi took
the position that it was neutral. From the outset, both Mencius
and Gaozi accept as a premise that human nature (*xing* 性) and
water are like phenomena:

> Gaozi said, "Nature is like a bubbling spring. If you make a
> channel for it to the east, then it will flow eastward. If you
> make a channel for it to the west, then it will flow west-
> ward. Human nature is not biased toward good or bad; it is
> like water which is not biased toward east or west."
>
> Mencius said, "Water certainly is not partial to east
> or west, but is it not partial to above and below? Human
> nature being good is like water going downwards. Among
> people, there are none who have [as their nature] not being
> good; of water, there is none which does not descend. Now,
> supposing water is splashed and made to jump up; it can be
> made to go higher than the forehead. Or, it can be made to
> stay on a mountain if it is banked up and caused to circu-
> late. How could this be the nature of water: it is like that
> because it is induced. Men can be made to do what is not
> good: their nature is still the same." (VIA.2)

The logic of this passage reflects an assumption shared by both
philosophers about the relationship of natural and human phenomenon. Both Gaozi and Mencius begin with the premise that
water and human nature are comparable and operate according
to the same principles. Thus, a proper understanding of the principles that guide the natural phenomenon implies an equivalent
understanding of those that guide human nature.

This passage has often been analyzed as an example of rhetorical technique and many scholars have pointed out the logical
limitations of argument by analogy, the primary rhetorical technique in early Chinese texts. If one regards the argument as
simply a rhetorical contrivance, then the argument is indeed
meaningless. However, if my hypothesis is correct—that early
Chinese philosophers assumed that the same principles informed

natural and human phenomenon—then Mencius' argument is both powerful and logical. Mencius won his argument with Gaozi not for the trivial reason that his rhetoric was more ingenious than that of his opponent, but *because he had a better understanding of water than Gaozi*. Mencius—unlike Gaozi—truly understood water; therefore, he knew that, just as water goes down, human nature tends toward the good.

We have already noted Mencius' admonition that the ruler should direct his people like the great Yu directed water. Water's innate tendency to move downward is also an important attribute in understanding the manner in which a true king attracts the allegiance of the world's people in the philosophy of Mencius. The key term when people respond to the attraction of a true king is *gui* 歸, often translated as to "return" or "turn to." In the *Mencius*, the true king is defined as one who practices the virtues of humaneness and rightness. Such a king will inevitably unite the people of the world under his rule because they will spontaneously "turn to" him, like water going downward:

> The people turning to (*gui* 歸) humaneness is like water going downwards or animals fleeing to the wilds. (IVA.9)

People turning to humaneness is thus a natural process, no different in kind than water going downward. It is the inevitable consequence of a humane ruler assuming rule.

In the above passage, Mencius uses *gui* for the people "turning to," that is, giving allegiance to, a humane ruler. *Gui* also means to return home. Here, however, the people are clearly giving their allegiance for the first time to a newly established king, rather than returning to him. The character is made up of two semantic elements, a foot (止) and a woman (帚) and a phonetic element that signified the sound of the word (自). *Gui* is also the verb used to describe a woman going to live with her husband's family after marriage, as was the accepted practice in ancient China, and this is the explanation for the character given in the *Shuowen* dictionary.

In the contexts of rivers, *gui* 歸 means the movement of a tributary stream toward a larger channel or that of a river toward

a. This sense is a clue to understanding why the people
ie true king: the people who turn to a true king (or a woman
who goes to her husband's home after marriage) are following
their innate tendencies. Their course, like returning home, is a
natural one. Thus, *gui,* which describes how water that spontaneously moves downward flows toward a larger body, can also be
used to describe how people turn their allegiance to the true
king. The implication is that both are inevitable, natural acts.

The metaphoric image of people going to the good ruler, like
water going downward is not particular to Mencius or the Confucian school. It also occurs, for example, in the *Mozi.* Here, the
good ruler is not described as one who rules humanely, but one
who practices love without discrimination and mutual advantage:

> I consider that people going to [one in authority who advo-
> cates] love without discrimination and mutual benefit is
> comparable to fire going upward and water moving down-
> ward. It is not possible to prevent [such movement] in the
> world. Therefore love without discrimination is the way of
> sage kings and that in which kings, dukes and noblemen
> find peace. (IV, *Jian'ai xia* 17, p. 32)

In passages such as those cited above from the *Mencius* and *Mozi,*
the philosopher assumes that the movement of the water and
the allegiance of the hearts of the people are part of the natural
order. This order was called *tian ming* 天命, "the mandate of
heaven," or in its more general sense, the "natural order."

Mencius uses the same metaphor of people turning toward a
ruler like water flowing down to explain how a ruler can achieve
preeminence in the empire: "Of the shepherds of the people in
the world today, there is not yet one who is not keen on killing
people. If there was one who was not keen on killing people,
then all the people beneath the sky would crane their necks and
look towards him hopefully." This expression—craning necks and
looking forward hopefully—is a conventional phrase used to describe how people look for the gathering of rain clouds in a time
of drought. "If he were truly like this, then the people would
turn to (*gui*) him, like water pouring down, so copiously, how

could anyone restrain them!" (IA.6). Mencius' point here is that the movement of the people's allegiance in the direction of the man who acts with humaneness is a spontaneous and unpreventable movement, part of the natural order, just as water moves downward. Just as water will always go down, the people will always turn their hearts to the humane ruler.

That water moves down is no less important to the *Laozi*. Here, too, there is a political analogy between water moving downward toward the rivers and sea and the movement of the people drawn toward a ruler. And here again, there is a common assumption that the behavior of the people will be like that of water:

> The reason that the River and seas rule the hundred valley streams is that they are good at taking a lower position to them. This is why they are able to be king over the hundred valley-streams. This is why the sage who wishes to be in authority over the people always humbles himself in his speech. (*De 27*; 66)

What attracts the people to the sage in this passage from the *Laozi* is not goodness but humility: like the rivers that attract the mountain streams, the sage takes a low position. The sage/king can obtain authority in the human sphere by imitating moral principles derived from studying the movement of water; thus, the *Laozi* assumes that human behavior and the natural world behave according to common principles, just as *Mencius* did.

Elsewhere, the *Laozi* combines the metaphor of the river into which all streams flow, joining their courses, with a sexual metaphor in which the female, like the river, normally takes the lower position. Here, he reverses the conventional belief in the relative strength of male and female, taking the female as ultimately the strongest. The sage ruler should thus study the technique of the ultimately conquering female rather than that of the active male:

> A large state is the lower reaches [of a river]. It is the female of the world. It is the intercourse (*jiao* 交) of the world. The female always overcomes the male by means of stillness

(*jing*). It is because of her stillness that it is appropriate for her to take the position below. Therefore, a large state takes over a small state by taking the lower position [but] a small state, by taking the lower position, is taken by a large state. Therefore, the one by being lower takes over; the other being lower, is taken over. Therefore, if the large state wants no more than to nurture the people in common and the small state wants no more than to enter service, and both are to get their desires; then the large one appropriately takes the lower position. (*De* 20; 61)

The term stillness (*jing* 靜), which the *Laozi* equates with the female in this passage, is also a desirable attribute for the mind/heart that makes it reflective like water, as I will discuss below.

The inevitable movement of valley streams toward larger bodies of water is also mentioned in the following passage from the *Laozi* (*Dao* 32) :

When the way (*dao* 道) is in the world, [the people] are like the valley streams in relation to the Yangzi and the sea.

In the *Mencius*, this movement is part of the natural order (*tian ming* 天命); here, in the *Laozi*, it is called the *dao*.

Water Carries Detritus

Water is a carrier and waste is dumped into rivers. Thus, the "lower reaches" or the "downstream" of a river are a place where detritus accumulates.

In the *Laozi*, on the one hand, the large state was compared with the lower reaches of a river (*De* 20; 61). As water flows it takes waste matter with it that gathers in the lower reaches. Low, damp regions were also undesirable places to live. To the *Laozi*, however, the lower reaches, like so much else ordinarily despised, are not undesirable. Indeed, the highest good, which has already been defined in this passage as being like water, is said to "stay in places the multitude detest."

In the *Analects*, on the other hand, "lower reaches" (*xia liu* 下流) refers to the muck and mire which a gentleman, by definition, detests:

> Zi Gong said, "Even Zhòu's badness was not so extreme. That is why a gentleman dislikes dwelling in the lower reaches; all of the disgusting things in the world flow (*gui*) there. (XIX.20)

Zhòu here is the name of the last king of the Shang Dynasty, Zhòu Xin 紂辛 (not the Zhōu 周 Dynasty). Zhòu Xin was an archetypal bad ruler and the point of the passage is that the evil influence of his ministers and cronies was even more significant than his own evil nature. The same expression of disgust for "downstream" also occurs in another passage of the *Analects* (XVII.24), and it appears to have been a conventional attitude. This is undoubtedly one reason why the *Laozi* makes the contrary point with such insistence.

Soft and Weak, Yielding, and Uncontending

Water is soft (*rou* 柔) and weak (*ruo* 弱) and it always yields to the hard or strong. It always yields, never contends (*bu zheng* 不爭), but follows the path of least resistance. Yet it can overcome any obstacle set in its path and wear down the hardest stone.

As we have already seen, Mencius advised a ruler to govern by behaving like Yu in directing water, avoiding the obstacles. One of the most interesting attributes of water to the *Laozi* is that although water is the softest of all substances, it is nevertheless the strongest. Water will always yield when anything confronts it; it does not "contend" or "contest." However, it is never defeated by ceding to the hard. Indeed, it avoids damage and ultimately achieves victory:

> The highest good is like water. Water's goodness is that it benefits the myriad living things (*li wan wu* 利萬物), yet does not contend[10] and stays in places the multitude detests.

Therefore it approximates the way. . . . It is because it does not contend that it is without misfortune. (*Dao* 8).

Not contending is an important idea in the *Laozi* where it is recommended as a tactic for the weak—or apparently weak. We should note here, however, that the *Analects* also tell us that a gentleman does not contend, without tying this principle to the movement of water (see XV.22, III.7).

Water always yields, but conversely, water is the most penetrative of all substances and will ultimately wear down even the hardest of objects:

> There is nothing softer and weaker in the world than water; and yet in attacking the hard and strong, there is nothing which can take precedence over it. This is because there is nothing which can take its place. There is no one in the world who does not know that the weakness of water can overcome the strong, and its softness, the hard; and yet there are none who can put this into practice. This is the reason for the words of the sage: "One who accepts the disgrace of his state is called the master of the altars of earth and millet. One who accepts the misfortune of the state is the king over the world." (*De* 39; 78)

The political advice given here is not that of the Confucians, but once again, the ruler is advised to study the principles that govern the movement of water and to model his own actions accordingly. The disgrace to which the *Laozi* refers may be a reference to water dwelling "where the multitude" detests, low damp places or downstream where detitrus collects, as well as to the weakness and softness of water.

The *Laozi* further refers to water's uncanny ability to penetrate:

> The softest in the world runs over the hardest in the world. That which has nothing there (無有) enters where there is no space. This is how I know the benefit of doing nothing (*wuwei* 無爲). (*De* 5; 43)

I will discuss the term *wuwei*, which I have translated here as "doing nothing" as a philosophical concept in the following chapter. Here, we should simply note that "doing nothing" is that which water does when as the softest thing in the world, it runs over wears down the hardest stone.

Water Takes Any Shape

Water yields to the hard and strong and pursues any opening and so it will take the shape of any container that encloses it. This characteristic—the ability of water to take the shape of whatever contains it—signifies flexibility and suppleness, the ability of a person to adapt their actions to circumstance.

In Daoist texts, the ruler, especially the ruler who is in a weak position, should act like water, yielding to pressure and taking whatever shape is required of him. Xunzi, on the other hand, compares the ruler with the vessel. Here, the people become the water and they take the shape of whatever holds them.

> The ruler is the bowl; when the bowl is round, the water is round. The ruler is the basin, when the basin is square, the water is square. (12 *Jun Dao*, p. 162)

The king rules his people who are flexible like water in a container. Thus, it is he who is responsible for the manner in which they behave. If his rule is good, the people will behave in a moral fashion.

Still Water Becomes Level

Water when still, not only takes the shape of its container and becomes clear, it also becomes absolutely level.

We have already referred to this attribute more than once. It was part of the *Shuowen*'s definition and a passage from the *Zhuangzi* (V *zhong*, 13 *Tian Dao*, p. 457) also referred to the absolute levelness of water when it is still, which serves as a

standard for the carpenter. Similarly, when *Xunzi* explained why
the gentleman will always gaze at a great river, he equated the
levelness of water with the evenhandedness or fairness of law:
"Used as a level, it is always even, like law (*fa* 法)" (28 *You Zuo*,
pp. 390–91).

*Still Water Clears Itself of Sediment
and Becomes Reflective*

Water may be dense and murky, but still water releases its sediment, becoming clear and reflective.

Self-clarification is an important attribute of water. In a passage from the *Mencius* already discussed, Mencius quoted
Confucius pointing out the wisdom of a nursery rhyme to his
disciples—"The water of the Cang Lang River is clear, so we
may wash our capstrings; the water of the Cang Lang River is
dirty, so we may wash our feet," observing that the water "takes
the principle by itself (*zi qu zhi* 自取之), just as men invite insult
upon themselves" (IVA.8). This passage is often cited as meaning
that one should retire from office in a corrupt world.

The contamination of water in a stream is often attributed to
the contamination of its source. In this passage from the *Xunzi*,
the source of the river is equated with the ruler:

> Hence, the vessels [for the performance of the offering rites]
> and the calculations [for divination] are the stream (*liu* 流)
> of good government, not its fount (*yuan* 原). The ruler is
> the fount of good government. The officials guard over the
> calculations; the ruler nurtures the fount. If the fount is
> clear, then the stream will be clear. If the fount is dirty,
> then the stream will be dirty. Therefore, if the ruler is fond
> of the rites and rightness. . . . (12 *Jun Dao*, p. 159)

Thus, just as a stream depends on the quality of its source for its
purity, so too does good government depend on the purity of the
ruler.

When water is still, however, any extraneous matter settles
and it becomes clear and "empty" of sediment. According to the

50

Laozi (Dao 15): "He of old who was good at practising the way was fine and subtle, penetrating the mysterious, so deep that he could not be known . . ." And in the same passage:

> Murky, he is like muddy water; broad, like a river valley.
> The muddy, when still, soon becomes clear; the settled,
> being disturbed, soon comes to life.

Stagnant water, however, may not be able to clear itself, as this late (syncretist) chapter from the *Zhuangzi* (VI *shang*,15 *Ke Yi*, p. 544) tells us: "The nature of water is to become clear when it is not disturbed, to become level when nothing moves it. But when it is blocked up and cannot flow, it also cannot become clear."

When water is still and clear, it becomes reflective. According to the *Zhuangzi* (II *xia*, 5 *De Chong Fu*, pp. 192–93), "No one takes flowing water as a mirror and yet he finds his reflection in the standing water of a *jian*-mirror." From as early as the Shang Dynasty, vessels filled with water were used as mirrors in religious rituals. These were called *jian* 鑒 or 監—the early form of the character lacks the metal radical (金). Originally, the character depicted a person kneeling before a vessel, his head bowed to look at his reflection:

Jian were buried with the dead, as well as used in ritual, so what one saw in such mirrors was more than simply a physical reflection.

The power of mirrors to reflect truths or principles rather than simple images is evident, for example, in the *Book of Songs*, as quoted by the *Mencius* (IV.2): "The mirror (*jian*) of the Yin [Shang] was not far off; it was in the rulers of the Xia." In other words, the mirror of the Xia rulers would show that the oppressive last ruler of the Shang would meet a similarly calamitous fate. Bronze mirrors, *jing* 鏡, in which metal rather than water serves as the reflector, did not become common until the Spring and Autumn Period (722–481 B.C.), although isolated examples occur as early as the Shang Dynasty. The two terms for mirror are sometimes

Figure 5. The Waving Surface of the Autumn Flood, by Ma Yuan, Song Dynasty (960–1126). *Imperial Palace Museum, Beijing, China. Photograph Courtesy of Wenwu Press.*

Figure 6. Clouds Rising from the Green Sea, by Ma Yuan, Song Dynasty (960–1126). *Imperial Palace Museum, Beijing, China. Photograph Courtesy of Wenwu Press.*

interchanged in the early texts, suggesting a common significance, and both were buried with the dead. The following passage from the *Zhuangzi* includes references to both *jing* and *jian* as a pair, perhaps not clearly distinguished from one another.

This passage is from the outer chapters of the *Zhuangzi* which A. C. Graham has classified as syncretist. The mind/heart at rest is compared with water which becomes empty of sediment (*xu* 虛) when still:

> When water is still, it reflects one's beard and moustache clearly. Its levelness corresponds to the carpenter's level (*zhun* 準) and the great craftsman takes his standard from it. If water, when still, is so clear, then how much more the quintessential spirit (*jing shen* 精神). The mind/heart (*xin*) of the sage is clear! It is the *jian*-mirror of heaven and earth and the *jing*-mirror of the myriad living things. . . . (V *zhong*, 13 *Tian Dao*, p. 457)

The term *zhun*, meaning level or standard, is that which the *Shuowen* used to define water.

Water's ability to empty itself of sediment when still and thus become reflective is particularly important in Daoist conceptions of the mind/heart (*xin* 心) and the terms still, *jing* 靜, empty, *xu* 虛, clear, *ming* 明, are all important in Daoist descriptions of the mind/heart, as I shall discuss in the following chapter.

Water Is Difficult to See

When water is empty of sediment, it becomes invisible. Although the ability of clear water to reflect is important in our texts, they reveal little interest in its transparency. Nevertheless, the point is made that when one looks at a large body of water, it is difficult to make out its substance. This is the subject of this passage from the *Mencius*:

> There is an art of looking at water. Always look at the ripples. When the sun and moon shine, the radiance will always illuminate them . . ." (VIIA.24)

Water which is transparent and vast beyond ordinary human comprehension is likened here to the wisdom of the sage; if we concentrate on the reflected light, however, we may discern the water in a great river or the sea or catch a glimpse of the wisdom of the sage.

Mountains and Rivers

Shui, as we have seen, means both water and river. Rivers and mountains often occur together as a cosmological pair, referring to ideas which we would discuss in terms of time and space.

The association of rivers with what we call the passage of time is most striking when rivers are paired with mountains. Mountains are the most permanent of natural phenomena, whereas river water continually passes by. Mountains are static; rivers move. Both endure through the generations. Mountains stand for what is permanent; rivers for transience—but also for continuity because their water (which flows from a spring) is continually replenished.

Physically, mountains and rivers are a complementary pair, like fire and water. Together, they embody both time and space. Mountains rise toward the sky, whereas water descends into the earth. Mountains are high; rivers, low. The oracle bone inscription forms of the character for spring, *quan* 泉, are pictographs of water flowing from a mountain cave:

This suggests the symbiotic relationship of mountains and rivers which find their source in mountain springs. Mountains and rivers together signify the whole cosmos.

From the earliest times, rivers and mountains were the objects of ritual offerings. Shang Dynasty oracle bone inscriptions frequently contain divinations about the offerings to various rivers and mountains. The Yellow River was the most powerful river spirit in these inscriptions, called simply the "River." The most powerful mountain was called simply the "Peak," most likely Song Shan in Henan Province, which later became the

Central Mountain of the five sacred mountains to which the emperor made an annual sacrifice from Han times on.[11] Popular methods of offering sacrifice to these nature spirits mentioned in the oracle bone inscriptions included the burning (rising?) and drowning (descending?) of animal and human victims.

The practice of making offerings of animals to the spirits of mountains and rivers continued in later times and Confucius makes a passing reference to this type of ritual in the following passage:

> The master said to Zhong Gong, "If the calf of a cow used for ploughing had a sorrel coat and good horns, though we would not wish to offer it in sacrifice, would the spirits of the mountains and rivers reject it?" (*Analects* VI.6)

Confucius was primarily concerned with ritual correctness as a formal means of ordering social relationships and avoided discussion of the supernatural implications of ritual content. Mozi, who led a rival school of thought to the Confucians in the fourth century B.C., advocated belief in the spirits of the mountains and rivers as a means of frightening people into behaving well even in out of the way places.[12] However, except for this passage from the *Analects*, the early Confucian and Daoist texts show almost no interest in rivers and mountains as spiritual objects.

As we have already seen, according to the *Analects*: "The intelligent find joy in water" whereas "the humane find joy in mountains." Thus, "the intelligent (*zhi zhe* 知者—those who understand or know) are lively and the humane (*ren zhe* 仁者) are still. The intelligent are happy and the humane, long-lived" (VI.22). In the Confucian ethic, *ren*, 'humaneness' or 'benevolence' is the most important of all virtues, the fullest expression of being human. This concept is related to the plant metaphor, as we shall see in Chapter 4. To be 'intelligent' or 'have understanding' (*zhi*) is a stepping stone in the achievement of humaneness—as Confucius tells his disciples elsewhere: "If he does not yet have understanding (*zhi*), how could he succeed in being humane?" (V.19), but intelligence is not in itself sufficient. Indeed, to Confucius, it may even be suspect: "The humane find rest in humaneness, the intelligent find advantage in humaneness" (IV.2).

Later Chinese landscape painting used mountains and rivers to encapsulate the cosmos. In Chinese, landscape painting was called "painting of mountains and water" (*shan shui hua* 山水畫). Indeed there is no word for landscape as such. Occasionally, painters such as Ma Yuan (ca. 1190–1225 A.D.) who made twelve studies of water in various forms, chose water itself as a topic for painting (see figures 3–6). From these paintings and from others that depict a scholar meditating on a river which flows in front of him, we can see that the early tradition of contemplating water as a means of understanding the cosmos continued into later times.

Most landscape painting, as the name *shan shui hua* implies, depicted both mountains and water—lakes or streams which find their source in mountains. Such painting conventionally includes a man or some sign of human habitation, such as a house or hut, within a landscape of mountain and water. People are depicted naturally within the cosmos rather than given unusual prominence. The mountains and rivers allude to permanence and change; a person strolling among the mountains, a dwelling, or a skiff floating on a river, to the brevity and transcience of human life. In some paintings, a conifer, such as a pine, may play the role of the mountain, both for formal reasons and because evergreen trees such as these were symbols of longevity. Metaphorically, the pine tree also suggests the enduring moral qualities of the Confucian gentleman.

These depictions of human life within a landscape of mountains and water were the primary subject matter of medieval Chinese painting, just as biblical narratives were that of medieval European painting. Chinese landscape paintings, however, were not narrative; nor were they based on a text. The people who stroll in the landscapes of mountains and water are not individuals or mythical archetypes; indeed, they are usually anonymous and a story is not depicted. Rather, the people are placed within space and thus within time, as represented by the mountains and rivers.

That Chinese chose to paint anonymous individuals within a

natural landscape of rivers and mountains and Europeans, scenes from biblical narratives is significant. Both expressions may be regarded as the natural outgrowths of their particular conceptual schemes. On the one hand, the European concept of the individual—with a limited mortal life—and a transcendent God found its aesthetic expression in narrative literature and painting that illustrated particular scenes and individuals from that literature. The Chinese, on the other hand, intimated human mortality and the unavoidable passing of time by depicting a person within a cosmos symbolized by a landscape of mountains and rivers. Such painting is, however, a later development and beyond the scope of the present study.

Water and Fire

Water, which forms a cosmological pair with mountains, is also paired with fire.

Water is necessary for human life; fire, for human society. In ancient China, as elsewhere in the world, a constant source of water was the first requirement for any settlement; fire provided warmth, transformed the raw into the cooked, and was used to clear the fields in the slash-and-burn method of agriculture practiced at the time. The texts refer to these functions. Furthermore, although the texts frequently refer to flood and drought as natural calamities, allusions to fire and water as the necessities of life generally connote common, everyday things, lacking in value, rather than precious objects. The *Mencius* (VIIA.23) states: "Though people cannot live without water and fire, if you knock on someone's door in the evening seeking water and fire, there is no one who does not give it, as it is of the greatest sufficiency. With sages governing the world who ensure that pulses and grains are like water and fire, how could there be anyone who is not humane among the people?"

Paradoxically, however, water and fire are the most destructive of natural forces and the expression "water and fire" (*shui huo* 水火) more commonly refers to their capacity for harm than their benefits, that is, water and fire stand for the natural disasters of flood and fire (or drought) or simply for calamity. The *Analects* (XV.35) give vivid expression to the paradoxical power of water, which is the source of both life and death. Here, Confucius contrasted water and fire with humaneness (*ren*), the cardinal virtue in his philosophy:

> For the people, humaneness is more vital than water and fire. In the case of water and fire, I have seen people who have died from stepping into them, but I have never seen anyone who died from stepping into humaneness.

In this passage, *shui* means both water—that which one drinks—and a flood or a river in which one may drown. When Confucius concluded that humaneness (*ren* 仁) is like fire and water in its ability to nourish human life (the people), but superior because it does not share the paradoxical quality of danger, he placed the natural phenomena and moral qualities on a par with one another and compared them directly.

The complementary forces that imbue and define all life came to be known as *yin* 陰 and *yang* 陽 from the end of Warring States Period. Water is *yin* and fire, *yang*. At the most primary level, water and fire sustain human life; yet, conversely, they are potentially the sources of death and destruction. Since fire rises and water descends, they sometimes signify the high and the low. In this, they are similar to mountains and water, but fire and water are also cosmic forces. As such, fire and water are mutually destructive—water puts out fire and fire vaporizes water. In later *yin-yang* theory, this becomes a continuum of mutual conquest. The earliest reference to this capacity that I have found is the *Tuan* commentary of the *Yijing*, which states explicitly that fire and water extinguish one another.[13]

In the early philosophical texts, fire and water form a pair, but the texts do not refer to their ability to extinguish one another. Although there are no references in our texts to fire and water as mutually destructive forces, the more straightforward image of water extinguishing fire does occur. Thus, according to Mencius, "The humane overcoming the inhumane is like water overcoming fire. Those who act in a humane manner nowadays are acting as though they would put out the fire in a cartload of kindling with a bowl of water and then, when it is not extinguished, say water does not overcome fire" (VIA.18). In other words, the humane—if they are sufficiently so—will naturally be victorious over the inhumane, just as water overcomes fire. If it appears otherwise—that the humane rulers are not those who achieve the greatest success in the world, it is only because the ruler does not have enough humaneness, not that the principle is wrong.

Yin-yang theory took darkness, *yin* 陰, and light, *yang* 陽, as the names symbolic of the dual forces of the cosmos. Both of these terms were originally associated with landscape rather than fire and water. *Yin* is defined in the *Shuowen* as "dark" and as "the south of a river and north of a mountain." In other words, it refers to the shaded areas of a river valley and the term is conventionally used to describe dark valleys (*yin gu* 陰谷), clouds, and rain. *Yang*, on the other hand, is "high and bright" and the commentators to the *Shuowen* explain it as the south side or top of a mountain. Originally, then, the terms referred to landscape: to the dark, shaded valleys and bright mountain peaks.

When *yin-yang* theory was formulated around the third century B.C., various complementary pairs were correlated with one another and these two terms (*yin* and *yang*) became established as rubrics that subsumed all of the others, including water and fire, female and male, below and above, moon and sun. Before this time, however, water and fire were at least as central to Chinese dualism as *yin* and *yang*, and even after the theory was formulated they continued to play an important conceptual role.[14]

The first Confucian text to discuss fire and water in the abstract, as elements or forces in a theoretical system, is the *Xunzi,* which also refers in several chapters to *yin* and *yang* as theoretical terms.[15] Fire and water are similar because, although they are not living things and have no will, both of them move of their own accord. This appeared to make them unique. Both are described as unstoppable forces. The *Mencius* (IIA.6), for example, refers to the force of "fire when it has first ignited and a spring when it has first broken through (*da* 達)."

Xunzi, writing a little later than Mencius, is more interested in cosmological theory, in the nature of fire and water as opposed to living things. Thus, he claims that water and fire move because they both have something called *qi* 氣 (which I translate here as "vitality"):

> Water and fire have vitality, but not life. Grass and trees have life, but not cognisance. Birds and beasts have cognizance, but no sense of right and wrong. People have vitality, life, cognizance, and also a sense of right and wrong. Therefore, they are the most noble in the world. (9 *Wang Zhi*, p. 109)

The term *qi* is a critical one in early Chinese philosophy and I will discuss its meaning in some detail in the following chapter. The character, in its earliest form, denotes clouds and the concept seems to derive from water vapor (which is produced by fire acting on water). It also is closely associated with breath—and mist, the breath of the earth. When it is dense, it becomes solid, like ice; dispersed, it becomes intangible. It is often translated as "matter," as opposed to *shen* 神, "spirit" and in later theory it is said to be that which everything is made of. Here, however, *qi* seems to refer specifically to that force which gives vitality or animation to things, though not necessarily life, rather than to something that can be found even in inanimate things.

Water and fire were only associated with the terms *yin* and *yang* in the late Warring States Period. Although the *Xunzi* talks about *yin* and *yang* in cosmological terms and links fire and water as unique in having *qi* but no life, it does not specifically apply the terms *yin* and *yang* to water and fire. Of the texts that we are considering here, this development occurs only in a late section of the *Zhuangzi*, described by Graham as 'syncretic' (probably third century B.C.). Here, the two pairs are explicitly linked when lightning is described in terms of the mixture of water (*yin*) and fire (*yang*):

> When wood is rubbed against wood, then it catches fire. When metal is held together with fire, then it flows. When *yin* and *yang* are mixed together, then heaven and earth

are startled; there is thunder and rumbling thereupon and fire in the middle of water..." (IX *shang*, 26 *Wai Wu*, p. 920)[16]

Thus, fire in the middle of water is lightning, here described as produced by the mixture of *yin* and *yang*.

Yin and *yang* are principles that refer to the physical world, to valleys and mountains or water and fire. They may also be applied to human society where they refer to such aspects of human life as female and male or subject and ruler. This holistic approach is the same as that which allowed philosophers from Confucius onwards, to discover principles applicable to human society in the behavior of water and other natural phenomena. They were not simply interested in the fact that water flows downward spontaneously, clarifies itself when still, yields to the hard, but wears down stone, and so forth as physical science. These were manifestations of universal principles. If they could properly understand these principles, then they could use them in governing the world and bringing order to it, or simply in fulfilling their personal potential.

In such a system, the right way for a person to behave is that which accords with the way of nature. Moral principles are not based on the commands of a transcendent being, that is, there are no moral imperatives. Nevertheless, there are principles of ethical behavior and concepts which embody these principles. Some such concepts will be examined in the following chapter.

Chapter 3

The Way and Other Ideas

The Way that can be told is not an unvarying way.
—Arthur Waley, *The Way and Its Power*

The Way that can be spoken of is not the
constant way.
—D. C. Lau, *Lao Tzu: Tao Te Ching*

The course which can be discoursed is not the
eternal course.
—Alan Watts, *Tao: The Watercourse Way*

Lodehead lodehead-brooking : no forewonted
lodehead
—Peter A. Boodberg, *Selected Works*

The Way can be spoken of, but it is not the
constant way.
—D. C. Lau, *Lao-tzu: Tao Te Ching,
Translation of the Ma Wang Tui
Manuscripts*

The right method of philosophy would be this.
To say nothing except what can be said. . . .
—Ludwig Wittgenstein, *Tractatus
Logico-Philosophicus* 6.53

Figure 7. Thatched Cottage among
Clouds and Trees, by Wang Fu, Ming
Dynasty (1366–1644). *National Palace
Museum, Taipei, Taiwan, Republic of
China.*

In the previous chapter, we saw that water in early Chinese philosophical texts has a number of attributes: it is a source of life, but it should flow in channels. If it breaches its channels and inundates the land, the result is death and destruction. Rivers, with a spring as their source flow continuously whereas a downpour of rain briefly revives plants, but dries up quickly and cannot continue to nourish them. Water always tends downward and it follows its downward course spontaneously. Water, which is soft, weak, and uncontending, yields to any hard object, but it will eventually wear down the hardest of stones and overcome any obstacle put in its path. Streams, on the one hand, carry detritus that collects down river. Still water, on the other hand, empties itself of sediment which settles at the bottom, so that it becomes clear and reflective. Water will take the shape of anything in which it is placed and it is perfectly level when it is still. In Chinese cosmology, water may be paired with mountains or with fire.

When water was discussed by the philosophers, they derived principles from the behavior of water, which they also ascribed to human conduct. Many abstract philosophical concepts in early Chinese texts are described in the same terms as water and share its attributes. They include some of the most fundamental ideas in Chinese thought, such as *dao* 道, conventionally translated as the "way," *wuwei* 無爲, "doing nothing," *xin* 心, the "mind/heart," and *qi* 氣, "breath" or "vitality." In this chapter, I will argue that this is not accidental, that these concepts share language with water because the abstract ideas were grounded in water metaphor. Many concepts are also grounded in plant metaphor, as I will discuss in the following chapter.

A comprehension of the implicit imagery of particular concepts also reveals the logic of their relationships. The recognition that an abstract concept is grounded in a concrete model not only clarifies the meaning of that concept, it elucidates its potential range and scope. Moreover, those concepts that are grounded in the same root metaphor are structurally related, but this relationship is not necessarily apparent at the level of the abstract terms. Indeed, it is only by gaining a grasp of the imagery that underlies these concepts that we can begin to shed some of the preconceptions that obscure understanding of the early Chinese conceptual scheme and thus the meaning of the arguments made by particular philosophers.

The "Way" (Dao 道)

Dao [*tao*[1]] conventionally translated as the "way" is one of the earliest and most important philosophical terms in ancient China. *Dao* was such an important concept in the *Laozi Daodejing* and *Zhuangzi* that the school of thought which centered on these two works came to be known as Daoist (*Dao jia* 道家) in the Han Dynasty. However, both *dao* and the closely related concept of *de* 德, conventionally translated as "virtue," were also key philosophical terms in the *Analects* of Confucius, and from Confucius' frequent use of the terms, we can see that they had already been established as the common currency of philosophical debate.

In his introduction to the *Analects*, D. C. Lau states, "The Way seems to cover the sum total of truths about the universe and man, and not only the individual but also the state is said either to possess or not to posses the Way. . . . [The way] is a highly emotive term and comes very close to the term 'Truth" as found in philosophical and religious writings in the West. . . .[2] Graham, on the other hand, notes "if we ourselves would prefer to think of it as absolute reality, that is because our philosophy in general has been a search for being, reality, truth, while for the Chinese the question was always, Where is the Way?'. . ."[3]

Although no translation of *dao* will be fully congruent with the Chinese concept, the conventional translation of the "way" is a fortuitous one. *Dao*, like "way," can be used in the specific sense of a way along which one travels—a road, path, or channel of water—and with the extended meanings of a way of doing something and the way that something happens. I shall argue in the following that the philosophical concept of *dao* as a natural course or way is grounded in the root metaphor of a stream of water. As we have already seen, one of the characteristics of water is that it flows in channels. In the early Confucian texts—the *Analects* of Confucius and the *Mencius*—the *dao* is more narrowly modeled on the channel or course. From this idea of the *dao* as a stream, its channel acting as a conduit which guides people in their actions, the idea of *dao* is extended to encompass a condition in which everything follows its natural course. In the *Laozi* and the *Zhuangzi*, *dao* is modeled not only on the stream and its course, but on the water itself in all its various manifestations. With this expanded imagery, the way also incorporates the idea of time which is, as we have already seen, expressed with water imagery.

Many Western scholars have used the metaphor of a road to explain the meaning of *dao*. In *Confucius: The Secular as Sacred*, for example, Herbert Fingarette makes extensive use of the road metaphor to explain the concept of *dao* and even describes the rites, *li* 禮, as the "road system" of the *dao*. In modern Chinese, the compound *daolu* 道路 means road and roads are certainly included within the category of *dao;* the same combination of characters also occurs in classical Chinese with the meaning of road (e.g., *Analects* IX.12) and road is one of the meanings of *dao* in Zhou Dynasty bronze inscriptions. Yet, as Fingarette himself observes, the metaphor of a road is not entirely apt for the philosophical concept because neither the doctrine nor the imagery associated with *dao* allows for the choice implied by a crossroad.[4] Furthermore, the way that is the *dao* flows in a single direction.

The reason for this lack of congruity is that *dao* does not have the specific sense of 'road': it is a general category in Chinese that encompasses waterways, roads, and various channels, all of those paths or "ways," which one may go along, moving by water as well as on land. If we take the metaphoric root of *dao* as a roadway, it is a peculiar road that moves in a single direction and has no junctions; but there is no longer any peculiarity if we take the natural course of a stream or waterway as the prototype for the concept rather than a road.[5] Although a waterway may be joined by tributaries, it has a source and flows in one direction, moving ever downward until it eventually reaches the sea.

The interpretation of *dao* as 'road' is appealing and understandable because roads are familiar metaphysical images in the

West. Its resonances range from the "road to Damascus" to the modern road movie, and so we readily respond to the road as a potentially profound image. But the interpretation of *dao* as a road is appealing for the very same reasons that it is misleading: roads tend to connote spiritual journeys to us, travels in the course of which people have encounters and experience various travails resulting in enlightenment or self-realization. We tend to *find* something on the road, be it God or ourselves. The *dao*, however, has no connotations of spiritual encounter or self-awakening. It is a course that one follows naturally. A person does not encounter God or the inner self by following the *dao*, but fulfils his highest potential as a human being. The person who follows the *dao* is simply the most fully human.

Before turning to the philosophical concept *dao* 道, as the term appears in the Chinese texts, let us look briefly at the etymology of the character. As Roger Ames (and Peter Boodberg) have observed, characters with the signific 辶 which denotes movement are normally verbs.[6] Furthermore, in the *Shang shu* (*Yu Gong*), *dao* is used as a verb, meaning to cut a channel for a river.[7] Such a channel "leads" or "guides." This verbal usage is often signified in writing by the character 導 (with a hand at the bottom) as opposed to *dao* 道, the character usually used for the noun, the 'way'). However, the two characters 道 and 導 had the same pronunciation (as they still do in modern Mandarin) and they were interchanged in the *Shang shu* and other early texts.[8] Indeed, as we shall see below, the verbal usage of *dao* is still retained in the *Analects*.

The character *dao* appears in Western Zhou bronze inscriptions as:

In the bronze inscriptions, there is no clear distinction between the verbal and nominal forms of the character. The earliest bronze form (a) is made up of a head: 首 (an eye with a brow):

and a signific element that is used in many verbs associated with movement: 行 (a picture of a crossroads, hence a road or way):

Sometimes, a foot 止: 𣥂 or a hand 又: 彳 may be added at the bottom of the character (b and c). When the foot and the left side of 行 are combined, they become the archaic form of 辶 (d). This is the origin of the modern character 道, the "way." However, in some forms of the character, the hand element 又 is retained and the thumb marked with a short stroke so that it becomes 寸 in the modern script. This is the origin of the verbal form 導, meaning to lead, guide, or conduct (e). The *Shuowen* dictionary mentions another ancient script form of the character, no longer used, which is made up of the head and the hand, but lacks the movement signifier 辶: 尊. This is probably another antecedent to the verbal form of the character now written as 導.

The definition in this dictionary takes the word's literal meaning of a course along which one travels to define its philosophical sense:

> The course which one goes along (*suo xing dao* 所行道) is the way (*dao* 道). It comes from 辵 [modern form: 辶, to move, pass by]. Once [something] comes out (*da* 達), it is called *dao*.

Da 達 which I have translated here as "come out" also means to "penetrate" or "break through"; it is used in this sense for both sprouts and springs which "break through" the earth. Thus, for example, the *Mencius* referred to a spring when it first breaks through (*da* 達) as an unstoppable force (IIA.6).

As a verb, *dao* can also mean to "speak" or "tell," as in: "the way (*dao*) can be told (*dao*), but it is not the constant way (*dao*)" (*Laozi, Dao 1*). This is not a verbal form of the noun "way," but a phonetic borrowing; that is, the verb, to tell, was written with a character first created to represent an unrelated word of the same sound. As Cao Dingyun has observed, an ancestral form of the character *dao* occurs in oracle bone inscriptions where it is most often used in this sense of "tell." In these inscriptions, the character has a man (亻) rather than the head which replaced it in the Zhou inscriptions. A foot: 止 or a mouth: 口 (ㅂ) may be added at the bottom to distinguish one homonym from the other.

Of particular interest to us here is that another character, usually transcribed as *yong* 永, which means to move on water rather than on land, also occurs in the oracle bone inscriptions in very similar contexts to *dao*. This character has water on the right side. The mouth may also be added at the bottom:

Their usage suggests that the two characters, one representing movement on land, the other movement on water, may have been variants of one another in the oracle bone inscriptions.[9]

The Analects and the Mencius

The character *dao* occurs over one hundred times in the *Analects*. It is most frequently used as a noun, but it also occurs as a verb meaning to "lead" or "guide" in a manner which may be associated with the early meaning of cutting channels to guide water:

> The Master said, "guide (道) them with administrative policy and keep them in order with punishment and the people will take action to avoid [punishment] but be without shame. Guide them by virtue (*de* 德) and keep them in order by [practice of] the rites (*li* 禮) and the people will have a sense of shame and reform themselves. (*Analects* III.3)

Here, then, as a verb, *dao* means to lead or guide the people along a course—of action—that will be natural to them. When *de,* "virtue," and training in the rites are used to guide them, it is a channel within which they will naturally stay without the threat of force.

70

When *dao* occurs as a noun in the *Analects*, it is used in two senses: one specific, the way of someone or something; and the other, general. As a specific term, *dao* usually has a modifier. For example, we find such phrases as "the way of a gentleman" (*junzi zhi dao* 君子之道), "the way of the former kings" (*xian wang zhi dao* 先王之道), and "the way of the Master" (*fu zi zhi dao* 夫子之道)—the way that Confucius advocated and personified. These "ways" are often thought to be prescriptive. However, the "way of the gentleman" is not the way that a gentleman *should* behave, but the way that anyone who can legitimately be called a gentleman (*junzi*)—literally "son of a lord" but an ethical term in the *Analects*—*will* behave; that is, the course of behavior that such a person will inevitably follow, just as a river will inevitably flow along its channel.

The same grammatical pattern, in which *dao*, the way, is modified by a noun that refers to a prototypical person or category of persons also occurs in the *Mencius*. Thus, for example, Mencius advocated that the ruler should follow "the way of a [true] king." If he follows this way, then all the people "under heaven" will "turn to" (*gui* 歸) him, just all streams flow toward the great rivers and all rivers flow to the sea. "Ways" are not always good; the *Mencius* also speaks of the "ways" followed by evil archetypes, such as the bad last kings of the Xia and Shang Dynasty, Jie and Zhou Xin, and the notorious Robber Zhi. These are the ways that such men of evil character inevitably follow, just as anyone who *is* a gentleman or a true king naturally and inevitably follows the course of action that is the "way of a gentleman" or the "way of a true king."

The Confucian cultivates his virtue or inner potency (*de* 德). From this source (which will not dry up like puddles after a rainfall), the way of the gentleman naturally flows. Thus, as Confucius' disciple, Youzi stated, "A gentleman tends the roots (*ben* 本); when the roots are established, the *dao* is generated. Filial love and brotherly devotion are the root of enacting humaneness" (*Analects* I.2). Although the primary metaphor here is a plant—the way is what happens when the plant of humaneness grows from the root of filial love and brotherly devotion—a spring, the source of a stream, as we have already seen, is also described as its "root." Here, then, we have a convergence of water and plant metaphors, with the stream of water regarded as a living thing, like a plant.

A gentleman will also take the way as his course. For example, according to the *Analects* (IV.9, VII.6), "The nobleman sets his mind on the way" (*zhi yu dao* 志于道—the meaning *of zhi* will be discussed later, see p. 86). The same expression is used in the *Mencius*. The passage (VIIA.24) that began, "There is an art of looking at water. Always look at the ripples. When the sun and moon shine, the radiance will always illuminate them" continues:

> As for the sort of thing that flowing water is, it does not move until it has filled the hollows. As for the way along which the gentleman sets his mind (*zhi*), he does not break through (*da* 達) until he succeeds in accomplishments.

I have translated *da* here as "break through" because this term is used for a spring when it first breaks through the surface of the earth (after which it cannot be stopped, like fire when it is first ignited). Here, the way that directs the gentleman's mind is like a stream of water. This "way" may be interpreted in a general sense, as that which D. C. Lau likens to "truth" in our conceptual scheme, or it could simply be the way of a gentleman.

Dao can also be modified by *you* 有, or *wu* 無. Classical Chinese does not have an existential verb equivalent to the English verb to "be." *You* means "there is," to "have" or "be there"; *wu* means "there is not," o "not have," "be without," or "not be there." When *dao* is modified in this manner, it may indicate a specific course or channel to be followed, as in: "For obtaining the world, there is a way" (*de tianxia you dao* 得天下有道, *Mencius* IVA.9). Although this usage of *dao* is similar to the English usage of way in the sense of method, that "method" is to follow a course that flows naturally. In the *Mencius*, when you follow the course of a true king, the people will turn to you, like water flowing downward, and you will obtain the allegiance of all under heaven.

The statement that "there is" or "there is not" *dao*—without a modifier—is sometimes a general statement of metaphysical import. In such cases, the topic of the sentence is usually *tianxia* 天下. I have been translating *tianxia* as "the world" in this context because it meant the entire known world, that over which the true king would exercize sovereignty. Literally it means "under the sky" or "under heaven," i.e. the earth that was inhabited by people. For example, in the *Analects* (III.24), Confucius says, "The world has been without the way for a long time." Alternatively we might translate this line as "Under heaven, there has been no way for a long time." To say that the earth is without the way means that the world is in disorder because there is no true king ruling it.

Here, we may remember the myth of Yu controlling the flooding waters by dredging out the riverbeds and channeling the flooding water so that it flowed into the sea. As S. F. Teiser has already pointed out, the flood is water out of place, a metaphor for social disorder in the world.[10] Yu guided the water according to its natural tendency to flow in channels. To *dao* is to cut channels or guide along them. When the world has no river channels, the water flows in every direction, making civilized life impossible. When it "has no *dao*," there is disorder. Heaven may use Confucius as "wooden clappers" (III.24) announcing that the way will soon "be there," but there must be a king who is humane and has a sense of right and wrong to guide the people along the proper channels. And when "there is *dao* under the sky/heaven," there will be order, channels of proper behavior established by a humane king, as the people "turn to" the man who follows the way set by heaven.

The *Laozi* and the *Zhuangzi*

In the *Analects* and the *Mencius*, there will be *dao* under the sky/heaven, when there is a ruler who has its mandate (*tian ming* 天命). Sky/heaven controlled the seasons, both those of the natural world and those of human society, as we have already seen (see pp. 20–22) and heaven's mandate signified the change in a dynasty after the inevitable decline of the previous lineage. In the Confucian texts, on the one hand, the true king

73

followed the way of the sky/heaven. In the Daoist texts, on the other hand, the *dao* takes precedence as a principle which is manifested in the movements of heaven, earth, and man. Here, the imagery associated with the *dao* is expanded from that of a way, watercourse, or even a river system to include the water itself, the substance in all its various manifestations and thus, the principle that lies behind water's many transformations— and those of everything else in the cosmos. This includes what we call time.

Let us first look at the *Laozi*. Here, sky/heaven is paired with earth, often in a male/female relationship, as part of the cosmos. The governing principle of that cosmos is called *dao*. As an abstract principle, the idea of *dao* here is grounded in water, not simply in the form of a waterway, but more generally in water with all its manifold properties. This may be seen both by direct comparisons in the text of *dao* with water and in the use of imagery associated with water to describe the *dao*.

Water, which runs in channels, provides life for agriculture; thus it is said to "benefit" (*li* 利). The *dao* also "benefits":

> The highest good is like water. Water's goodness is that it benefits the myriad living things (*li wan wu* 利萬物), yet does not contend and dwells in places which the multitude detest.[11] Thus, it approximates the Way (*ji hu dao* 幾乎 道). (*Dao* 8)

Here, the *dao* is a general term, rather than specifically the way of heaven, and it is directly compared with water. The *wan wu*, as I will also discuss again below, are all living things: plants, animals, and people.

Thus, the *dao* benefits all living things, just as water nourishes life. The analogy of *dao* and a water channel, both of which nourish life is made explicit in the following: The *dao* is the watercourse (*zhu* 注) for the myriad living things (*De 21*; 62). *Zhu*, which I have translated here as "watercourse" might in this context also be translated as "irrigation channel." *Zhu*, like *dao*, can also be used as a verb for making channels. Thus, when the great Yu controlled the flooding water: "Yu, dredging the nine rivers and clearing the paths of the Qi and Ta, made channels for (*zhu*) them to the sea; cutting out the [riverbeds of the] Ru and Huai and building up the banks of the Huai and Si, he made channels (*zhu*) for them to [flow to the Yangzi] River" (*Mencius* IIIA.4).

The *dao* as a watercourse, providing benefit for agriculture, is also implied in a following passage in which the ruler is advised to act like water, giving benefit to the people, but not claiming ownership over them:

> The *dao*, wending and weaving, can flow left or right.
> It achieves success and accomplishes its task, but we do
>   not call it "having."
> The myriad living things turn to it (*gui*), yet do not take
>   it as their ruler. (*Dao* 34)

The ruler who follows the *dao* is like a stream of water, a source for life but one which does not attempt to dominate.

The Confucian, on the one hand, texts tell us that under the sky/heaven, "there is" (*you*) or "there is not" (*wu*) *dao*, that is, the world is governed by a good ruler and so it is in order with everything following its natural course according to the seasons, or else there is a bad ruler and it is in disorder. The *Laozi*, on the other hand, states that the *dao* "is in" or "at" (*zai* 在) the world, that is, "under the sky/heaven." As in the Confucian texts, this implies a natural order:

> The *dao* being in (*zai*) the world is like the river valleys in
> regard to the [Yangzi] River and sea. (*Dao* 32)

In other words, when the *dao* is under sky/heaven, everything flows naturally toward it, just as the Yangzi and sea attracts the smaller rivers and streams of the river valleys.

The image of a stream that has a natural spring as its source is evoked elsewhere in the *Laozi*. Here, the *dao* is described as a source that can never be used up, just as one may take water from a spring but it continually replaces itself. That it is "empty" means that it is empty of sediment and thus clear:

The *dao* is empty, yet using it, it does not need to be refilled.
A deep spring (*yuan* 淵)—it seems like the ancestor of the myriad living things. (*Dao* 4)

Yuan, which I have translated as a "deep spring" here, is a common image in Chinese poetry and philosophy. It is conventionally translated as "abyss" because it connotes something that is mysterious and visually impenetrable, like "looking into an abyss." However, the Chinese term has a water radical and, although it is an abyss, it is an abyss that contains a spring of water. The *dao,* then, is like the water that comes from a deep spring, ceaselessly emerging from the depths of the earth, providing the source of life for the myriad living things.

And elsewhere in the *Laozi* (*Dao* 25), *dao* is described:

There is some thing forming in the murk (*you wu hun cheng* 有物混成).
So still, so deep!
Self-established, it does not change.
Going everywhere, it does not diminish.
It can be considered the mother of heaven and earth.
Not knowing its name, I call it "*dao.*"

Hun, which I translate here as "murk," is often translated as chaos or confusion. It implies the mixing of two substances, one clear and one dense, like water and dirt or the white and yellow of an egg, so that the substance becomes cloudy or opaque. As we have already seen, sediment settles in a still pond of water so that it becomes "empty" and clear. In the same manner of separation, "heaven" (i.e., the sky) is clear (*qing* 清); the earth, "muddy" or "dense" (*zhuo* 濁, *ning* 寧).[12] "Still and deep" further suggest a deep gorge or abyss in which the water is dark and impenetrable to the viewer, an image in these texts that conventionally suggests something unknown and mysterious.

Self-establishing (i.e., having no parents) and unchanging, the *dao* is like a stream with a natural spring. Going everywhere, but never in danger of running out, the mother of heaven and earth, the way is like a primeval water source. Water and the way are both transient and yet they pass by continuously. As we have seen, Confucius compared "what passes" (*shi* 逝) with the water of a river (*Analects* IX.17). This passage (*Dao* 25) from the *Laozi* continues:

> Not knowing its name, I call it "*dao*." If I am forced to give it a name, I say "great" (*da* 大). "Great" is called "passing away" (*shi* 逝).[13] "Passing away" is called "going far away" (*yuan* 淵). "Going far away" is called "going back" (*fan* 反).

The use of the term *shi* 逝 to describe that which passes by, what we call time, in the *Analects* and as a name for the *dao* in the *Laozi* is an important clue to the Daoist conception of the *dao*. In the *Laozi* and *Zhuangzi,* where the *dao* is the supreme principle in the cosmos, the course of the *dao* signifies passing time. The *dao* like water—and time—is amorphous, something that continually passes by, which may contain things but can never be grasped. That "going far away" is called "going back" or "returning" (*fan*) may refer to an idea that streams replenish themselves from the waters of the underworld, the Yellow Springs.

And the passage ends:

> Man models himself of earth.
> Earth models itself on heaven.
> Heaven models itself on the way.
> The way models itself on that which is so of itself (*zi ran* 自然).

The term *zi ran*, "that which is so of itself" is also used with reference to plants (see Chapter 4). Water that flows unwilled and plants that grow undirected are both "so of themselves."

> Like water, *dao* is amorphous:
> The *dao* as a [living] thing (*wu* 物) is vague, indistinct.
> Indistinct, vague,
> Yet within it are configurations.
> Vague, indistinct,
> Yet within it are living things (*wu*). . . . (*Dao* 21)[14]

Similarly, the way as a principle is something which cannot be expressed because such expression limits it: "The *dao* can be told, but it is not the constant *dao*" (*Dao* 1), or, in Alan Watts felicitous translation, "The course which can be discoursed is not the eternal course."[15]

The *Zhuangzi* stresses the amorphous aspects of the *dao* and here the *dao* clearly comes to incorporate that amorphous and ungraspable aspect of life: what we call time. In this text, people are often seen as being in the *dao*, but the *dao* is something vague and indistinct, something in which we exist, like fish in water, but cannot understand. The *dao* is thus like water itself rather than simply its course. It is something that "is there," but cannot be grasped, something that is shapeless and invisible:

> The *dao*, which has essence[16] and reality but does nothing (*wuwei* 無爲) and has no shape, can be transmitted, but cannot be received; can be obtained, but cannot be seen. (*Zhuangzi* III *shang*, 6 *Da Zong Shi*, p. 246)

Elsewhere in this chapter, people who are in the *dao* are likened to fish in water:

> When the spring has dried up, the fish stay together on the land, spitting on each other to provide moisture and foaming on each other to get wet. This is not as good as forgetting about one another in the rivers and lakes. Rather than praising Yao and condemning Jie, they [the sages] would be better to forget them both and transform themselves in the *dao* (p. 242).[17]

The *dao* is not only "in" or "at" the world, it is man's natural habitat, just as water is the natural habitat of fish.

And later on in the same chapter:

> Fish go to one another in water; men go to one another in the *dao*. As for those who go to one another in water, you nurture them by making a pond; as for those who go to one another in the *dao*, their life will be peaceful if they have no [official] duties. Therefore it is said, fish forget about

themselves in water; men forget about themselves in the *dao*. (p. 272).

People are to the way, then, as fish are to water. The dao nourishes and sustains them, but surrounded by the *dao*, we are unaware of our environment, just as fish are unaware of the water.

In sum, the prototypical images of the *dao* are a channel or watercourse, water that benefits all living things and the river system itself, the stream that never ceases, and the pond that clears itself of sediment. It is that which nourishes and encompasses us, but of which we are unaware. The Confucian texts stress its natural order; the Daoists, its transformations and amorphousness, but both interpretations of the concept find their root in the attributes of water.

"Doing Nothing" (Wuwei 無爲)

In a passage from the *Zhuangzi* translated above (III *shang*, 6 *Da Zong Shi*, p. 246), the *dao* was described as "doing nothing (*wuwei*) and having no shape." In the previous chapter, we also saw that water "does nothing" (*wuwei*), but even though it is the softest thing in the world, it will overcome the hardest (see p. 8). *Wuwei* is a key philosophical term in the Daoist texts and one of the most difficult to translate. If, however, we take water as the primary image on which the concept is modeled, its meaning becomes clear: *wuwei* is what water does; it has no will and does not act, but it moves spontaneously downward following the contours of the land and clears itself when it is still.

Wuwei may be translated as "doing nothing," "without action," or "without willful action." In the above, I have followed A. C. Graham's suggested translation "doing nothing" because it suggests a lack of intention in colloquial English. However, this translation is not congruent with the Chinese grammar. W*u* 無 (or 无) is the negative counterpart of *you* 有, "there is," to "have," "be there." Thus, it is variously translated as "there is not," to "not have," "be without," or "not be there." As a verb, *wei* 爲 means to "do" or "act" and suggests deliberate intention. Here, following the negative, *wu*, it should be a noun such as "acting" or "action." *Wuwei* means that there is no "acting" or "action." There is no action, but something nevertheless happens. As the *Laozi* states, "Doing nothing, there is nothing not done" (*De* 8; 48).[18]

The spontaneous movement of water downward was an important image in the *Analects* and the *Mencius*. However, this term is not found in the *Mencius* and occurs only once in the *Analects*:

> The Master said, "One who governed without acting (*wu-wei*) was Shun. Why act! He simply assumed a respectful demeanor and faced south." (*Analects* XV.5)

Although water is not mentioned in this passage, its sense can best be understood in terms of the water metaphor: Shun (like water) did not take any deliberate action, but his benevolence extended from him naturally, like water flowing from a spring. Or "a river breaching its channel so copiously that nothing can stop it," which is how Mencius described Shun's goodness after he had heard a single good word and witnessed a single good deed" (VIIA.16), perhaps harking back to this same passage. Although the term *wuwei* does not occur at all in the *Mencius*, the metaphor of water moving inexorably downward and tributaries flowing spontaneously toward the main artery and thus to the sea (*gui* 歸) is embedded in Mencius' idea of the manner in which the people will turn to the just ruler.

The term *wuwei* is so closely associated with Daoism (as well as with Legalism later on although this will not be discussed herein) that some scholars have suggested this passage from the *Analects* is a later interpolation rather than part of the original text. The prevalence of the imagery associated with *wuwei* in all texts, however, suggests that the idea—and perhaps the term itself—was not initially or exclusively Daoist, even though it became a key term in the Daoist vocabulary and was closely associated with Daoist philosophy.[19]

The *Xunzi,* which is somewhat later than the *Mencius* and draws on the Daoist tradition as well as the Confucian, does use the term *wuwei.* As we have already seen, in response to the question of why a gentleman always looks at the water of a great river, he explained: "Water extends everywhere and gives everything life without acting (*wuwei*)" (28 *You Zuo,* p. 390). Here, *wuwei* is specifically a description of what water does. As I shall discuss in the following chapter, Xunzi's use of the term *wei* 僞 to describe human artifice as opposed to nature (*xing* 性) may also be related to the use of the term *wuwei* in the Daoist texts.

Wuwei is particularly important in the *Laozi* where the strategy proposed to the sage ruler is, quite simply, to imitate water. Water does not "act," but it will clear itself of sediment and the plants that are nourished by it will grow of themselves. Similarly, the sage ruler should not "act" and his people will be transformed: "When I do nothing (*wuwei*), the people are transformed by themselves. When I am fond of stillness, the people act correctly by themselves. When I do not have official duties, the people are enriched by themselves. When I desire not to desire, the people are simple of themselves" (*De* 16; 57).

The true sage does not act. Those who engage in learning and practice official duties (*shi* 事) act deliberately but ultimately with futility. These are the philosophers, whose learning, as opposed to intuitive grasp of the way, is responsible for the decline of the world: "Those who practise studying augment [their knowledge] daily. Those who hear the way decrease [their actions] daily. They decrease them, and decrease them again, until they do nothing. Doing nothing (*wuwei*), there is nothing not done" (*De* 8; 48).

Imitating water by yielding—not taking any aggressive action—is also the means for the weak to defeat the strong: "There is nothing softer (*ruo* 弱) and weaker (*rou* 柔) in the world than water; and yet in attacking the hard (*jian* 堅) and strong (*qiang* 強) there is nothing that can take precedence over it" (*De* 39; 78). As we have already seen, it "does not contend" and seeks the lowest point; and so "that which is softest in the world will run over that which is hardest. That which contains nothing enters where there is no space. This is how I know that doing nothing (*wuwei*) is of benefit" (*De* 5; 43). "Doing nothing" is thus to be like water, soft and yielding, not contending or acting, but nevertheless a match for any opponent and able to overcome any obstacle.

"Not contending" (*bu zheng* 不爭) is an important aspect of "doing nothing." "The sage is without action (*wuwei*) and therefore without defeat" (*De* 23; 64). The Great River and sea take the lower position to the smaller rivers and streams and therefore act as their king. The sage ruler humbles himself before the people. Thus, "because he does not contend, there is none able to contend with him" (*De* 25; 66).

In the *Laozi*, not contending is a strategy for survival and eventual victory: one should be like water, which is weak but overcomes every obstacle by yielding to the hard. The Confucianists do not associate the principle of "not contending" with water in the same manner, but "not contending" is not specifically a Daoist principle. In Confucianism, yielding (*rang* 讓) is both a virtue and a key element of the conception of the rites (*li* 禮). A son will naturally yield to his father and anyone, to an elder. Thus, as we have already seen, filial love is the root of humaneness.

Similarly, neither the gentleman nor the true king will need to struggle to maintain their position. According to the *Analects* (XV.22), "The gentleman knows his worth and does not contend (*bu zheng* 不爭)." And elsewere (III.7): "There is nothing about which gentlemen [should] contend. When unavoidable, they use archery—bowing and making way for one another, they ascend. Coming down, they toast—their contention is that of gentlemen." In other words, it is mediated by the ritual of an archery contest. In *Mencius*, too (see Chapter 6), the true king does not need to engage in battle—there are no rivers of blood—because the people, including the army of his opponent, will turn their allegiance toward him (like water flowing downward).

Although the *Zhuangzi* (III *shang*, 6 *Da zong shi*, p. 246) did describe the *dao* as "doing nothing and having no shape," such theoretical discussion of the *dao* is uncommon elsewhere in the Inner Chapters of the *Zhuangzi*—the earliest section of the text. Nevertheless, intentionless movement is a common theme in these chapters. It is most frequently expressed by the term *xiao-yao* 逍遙, often translated as "roaming" or "wandering." Thus, the sage "roams freely" or "wanders" (*xiaoyao* 逍遙) in the *dao*, just as fish swim freely in a stream. This "wandering" is a mental activity, like the free movement of water, which wanders wherever it finds no obstacle.

Like *wuwei*, *xiaoyao* is to be free of conscious deliberation. There are two other textual references to "doing nothing" in the Inner Chapters. In both of these the two terms are associated with one another. Thus, the sage "wanders" in the wilderness of "doing nothing" (*xiaoyao hu wuwei zhi ye* 逍遙乎無爲之野) (III *shang*, 6 *Da Zong Shi*, p. 268); and having planted a useless tree in the realm of Nothing Whatever, "vaguely, does nothing (*wuwei*) beside it; [his mind] wandering (*xiaoyao*), he sleeps beneath its branches" (I *shang*, 1 *Xiaoyao You*, p. 40). These occasional references to *wuwei* suggest that although the term was known to the author of this section, it had not yet become significant as a technical philosophical term.

In the later sections of the *Zhuangzi*, especially those chapters that Graham calls "syncretist," *wuwei* is used more frequently, possibly because these chapters have been influenced by the terminology of the *Laozi*. One of water's important characteristics is that it becomes clear and reflective when still. When water is still it "does nothing" (*wuwei*):

> When water is still, it reflects one's beard and moustache clearly. . . . The mind/heart (*xin* 心) of the sage is clear! It is the *jian*-mirror of heaven and earth and the *jing*-mirror of the myriad living things. That which, empty and still (*xu jing* 虛靜), insipid and bland, silent and featureless, does nothing (*wu wei* 無爲) is the level [which acts as a standard for] heaven and earth and it is the culmination of the way (*dao* 道) and virtue (*de* 德).

Another characteristic of still water, as we have already seen, is that it is perfectly level and so it is the "standard" for a carpenter's level. The mind/heart should similarly be still and clear and it too can act as a standard in the world.

And the passage continues with an application of the principle of *wuwei* to the ruler:

> Therefore, the emperor, kings, and sages rest there. If they rest, then they become empty (xu 虚); if they become empty, then they are filled and that which fills them becomes ordered. If they are empty, then they are still; if they are still, then they move; if they move, then they succeed. If they are still, then they do nothing (*wuwei*); doing nothing (*wuwei*), those who undertake official duties take responsibility. (V *zhong*, 13 *Tian Dao*, p. 457)

The sage or ruler, thus, who "does nothing" has a mind which is "still" and "empty" (of sediment), so he perceives clearly the ordered relationships of that which fills his mind.

As this chapter continues, we see that *wuwei* is here both a technique and a philosophy of government:

> Doing nothing (*wuwei*), one has more than enough with which to make use of the world; doing something (*youwei* 有爲), one is insufficient for being used by the world. . . . Those above always do nothing (*wuwei*) and make use of the world; those below always do something (*youwei*) and are used by the world. . . . The sky/heaven does not generate, and yet the myriad living things are transformed; earth does not rear, and yet the myriad living things are nurtured. The emperor and king do nothing and yet the world achieves. . . .

Although it is beyond the limits of this study, this use of the term *wuwei*—as a technique of government by nonaction—is common in the *Hanfeizi*.

Wuwei, in sum, is what water does. Since water has no consciousness or will, it never "acts." Yet it moves, spontaneously bubbling up copiously from its source, flowing ever downward. Water always yields, but it overcomes all obstacles however strong or hard. When still, it spontaneously clears itself of sediment and becomes perfectly reflective. It does not act, but it nour-ishes all living things. If this imagery, then, is the root of the concept of *wuwei*, its meaning becomes clear. Furthermore, we can see that *wuwei*, which is what water does, is the supreme expression of the *dao*, which is also modeled on water.

The Mind/Heart (Xin 心)

In the passage translated above, the mind/heart (*xin* 心) was compared to a pond of water that becomes clear when still. *Xin*, as an organ, is the heart. This is clear from the original charac-ter which is a picture of a heart:

But it was the heart, rather than the brain, which was believed to think in ancient China. Thus, according to the *Mencius*, "The organs of the ears and eyes do not think (*si* 思) and they are beguiled by [living] things (*wu* 物). When [living] things have contact with one another, they simply attract each other. As for the organ of the mind/heart, it thinks (*si*). . . ." (VIA.15). *Si* 思—which I translate here as "thinking" refers to contemplation or meditation.

Si, "thinking," may be juxtaposed with either "learning" (*xue* 學) or with following one's desires (*yu* 欲). Desires are defined in this context as what our eyes and ears entice us to want. In our own conceptual scheme, however, rationality and emotion are conventionally opposed to one another. Reason is associated with the brain, emotion with the heart. There is no heart/mind di-chotomy in classical Chinese, but if we translate *xin* as "heart," our own conventions make it almost impossible to escape the habitual connotation of emotion, as opposed to reason. Indeed, *qing* 情, the word that means passions or emotions, does not acquire this sense until the Han Dynasty; in the early texts, it refers to one's natural endowment, but not specifically one's passions.[20]

Nor, as Fingarette has observed, is there a mind/body dichot-omy.[21] The *xin* is an organ of the body that thinks and feels. As such, it is what distinguishes people from animals. This is not only true in the *Mencius*, where the human heart is described as having "sprouts" (*duan* 端) that contain a person's potential for goodness (as I will discuss in the following chapter). Even in the *Zhuangzi*, the mind/heart is described as having the capacity to tell "what is" (*shi* 是) from "what is not" (*fei* 非), or right from wrong (I *xia*, 2 *Qi Wu Lun*, p. 56). A. C. Graham has objected to the translation "mind" for *xin* in pre-Han texts on the grounds that there was no distinction between mind and body before the Chinese scheme was influenced by Indian Buddhism. However, he also describes the *xin* as the organ with which one thinks and approves or disapproves—functions that we would attribute to the brain.[22] My rather awkward translation of mind/heart is meant to convey the idea that this is the physical organ with which one thinks, although that organ is the heart.

What then is this organ like; how was mind/heart conceived? The primary image for *xin* is that of a pool of water which is clear and reflective when still. When sympathetic emotion is stirred, the heart has a responding resonance.[23] Violent emotion is the stirring up of the *xin*—the calm pool—thus causing one's perception of reality—the reflection—to be blurred whereas the still, undisturbed mind, contemplates (*si* 思) with clarity. This disturbance is described in terms of *qi* 氣, "vapor" or "vital energy" (see below).

The mind/heart may also move or be moved in a certain direction. Deliberate movement of this kind is called *zhi* 志, conventionally translated as "will" or "intention." "The nobleman sets his mind/heart (*zhi*) on the way" (*Analects* IV.9, VII.6). This *zhi*, as Graham has already pointed out, is a cognate of *zhi* 之, to "go," to which a heart radical has been added. Thus, the nobleman moves his mind/heart along the course of the way.[24] Such movement of the heart is also implied when the people "turn to" or "give their allegiance" (*gui* 歸) to the ruler. As we have already seen, *gui* is used both for streams and tributaries turning or flowing to larger bodies of water, as well as people giving their allegiance. When the people turn to a ruler, it is because they "cause their hearts to turn [i.e., flow] to him" (*gui xin yan* 歸心 焉, *Analects* XX.1).

The mind/heart, then, is like a pool of water that settles when it is undisturbed, becoming clear and empty of sediment, but, like water, it may also move or be drawn in a certain direction. It may be directed, as in the case of the Confucian who will set his mind/heart (*zhi* 志) on a certain course, that of a gentleman or a true king. Or, the mind/heart may move freely, like water finding its own course by following the contours of the land, if "there is no action" and one "does nothing" (*wuwei*). In the case of the people, however, their mind/hearts are drawn to follow a certain course by the way that has been established for them, rather than moving of their own volition. Drawn by the way, they will inevitably go to a good ruler, like water flowing downward.

These movements of the mind/heart are those we describe in terms of will, intention, and emotion. Moral goodness is also located in the mind/heart. As we have already seen, Mencius argued that people's nature is good, just as water moves downward. Since the model for that nature, however, is one of plant life—seedlings or sprouts that grow naturally in the *xin*—it will be discussed in the following chapter.

"Breath," "Vapor," "Vital Energy" (Qi 氣)

According to the *Xunzi*, fire and water have *qi*, but do not have life, cognizance or a sense of right and wrong, as we have already seen. I translated *qi* as "vitality" in this context. The image of the mind/heart as something that may move in a certain direction, respond with a resonance, or clarify itself when it is still, is that of a stream or pond. It is not water *per se* that informs the mind/heart, however, but *qi*, a concept modeled on water. The primary model for the concept of *qi* is water in the form of vapor, but water vapor may disperse, liquefy as water, or solidify as ice. Thus *qi* encompasses not simply vapor but all the various forms that vapor may take including the liquid and the solid.

Qi is one of the most important—and one of the most difficult—of all early Chinese concepts to understand. In the West, the idea of *qi* has been introduced through the technique of *qi gong* [*ch'i kung*] in martial arts—the ability to control and use

87

one's breath or inner vitality (*qi*) to obtain great force or power—and in Chinese medical techniques, such as acupuncture, which is based on the idea of channels of *qi* moving through the body.

According to A. C. Graham, "*qi* . . . has the place in Chinese cosmology occupied by matter in ours. The basic metaphor behind the word matter is of timber (Latin *materia*), inert and cut up and to be assembled by a carpenter; *qi*, on the other hand, is in the first place the breath, alternating between motion and stillness, extended in space but insubstantial, although vaporizing to become visible on a frosty day. The *qi* is conceived as becoming solider the more slowly it moves, with the more tenuous circulating within and energizing the inert, for example, as the *jing* "quintessence," the vitalizing fluid in the living body. In its ultimate degree of fineness we could think of it in Western terms as pure energy."[25]

The *Shuowen* defines the character *qi* 氣 as "cloud vapor," which is consistent with the form of the character oracle bone and bronze inscriptions, although the character is used in the extant inscriptions as a phonetic borrowing for a word that is unrelated in meaning (乞). The earliest forms are:

$$\equiv \qquad \succeq \qquad \succeq$$

Clouds and rain form a cycle of ever renewed water.

In the modern character, the grain radical (米) has been added. It may, as the commentators explain, signify the steam of cooked food—or it might signify the essence of that food, that which is consumed by the ancestral spirits when it is given as an offering. An early form of the character, found on an inscribed jade thought to come from the Warring States Period, known as the "Moving Qi" (*Xing Qi*) jade, has a fire signific added. This suggests a prototypical image of clouds produced by sun on water or else of steam, that is, water vaporized by fire. Nevertheless, the *qi* that is the primary subject of the inscription is the human breath.[26]

The Moving *Qi* jade describes *qi* in a rhymed verse:

> The moving *qi* is swallowed;
> When it is swallowed it nurtures;
> When it has nurtured, it is expelled;

When it is expelled, it goes down;
When it goes down, it settles;
When it settles, it solidifies;
When it solidifies, it sprouts;
When it sprouts, it grows;
When it grows, it returns;
When it returns; then it [ascends to] sky/heaven.
As for sky/heaven, its root is in the above.
As for earth, its root is at the below.
If one follows along, one lives.
If one goes against, one dies.

Here, then, *qi* is both human breath and the cycle of water that nourishes all life, the ultimate life force.

The *qi* of earth becomes mist that forms in the evening and nourishes both plant life and the seedlings of goodness in the human heart, as we shall see in our discussion of Mencius' concept of human nature in the following chapter. In a human being, *qi* is literally breath, but it is also an abstract concept like vitality or energy. Thus, according to the *Xunzi*, fire and water have *qi*, but no life. The *qi* in people is closely associated with their mind/heart, but the mind/heart is both a physical organ that circulates blood and the organ with which one thinks and feels. Blood and *qi* are closely associated, but they are also distinct and when *qi* becomes a principle in medical theory, it moves along its own courses, which are not the same as the veins or arteries.[27]

Qi is the source of emotional behavior such as lust, aggressiveness, and greed. According to the *Analects* (XVI.7):

When one is young and one's blood and *qi* are not yet settled, one's guard is against lust. When one has reached maturity and one's blood and *qi* are firm, one's guard is against aggressiveness. When one has reached old age and one's blood and *qi* are in decline, one's guard is against acquisitiveness.

Similarly, the *Xunzi* (2 *Xiu Shen* p. 16), which advocated the rites as the ultimate means of cultivating character and controlling society, stated, "The art of controlling the *qi* and nurturing the mind/heart: If the blood and *qi* are firm and strong, then soften them with balance and harmony. . . ."

As I have already mentioned, one thinks (*si* 思) by stilling one's heart. Emotions are disturbances of one's *qi*. And one's breathing as well as one's heart are linked with such disturbances. Thus, in the *Mencius*, we find that "hurrying and stumbling, the *qi* in turn affects the mind/heart" (IIA.2). It seems to refer both to breathlessness and lack of emotional calm. Similarly, in the same passage, courage was discussed in terms of "not moving the mind/heart." The *Laozi* (*Dao* 10) also states:

> In concentrating your *qi* so that it is supremely soft, can you reach infancy? In cleaning and wiping the dark mirror (*xuan jian* 玄監), can you make it flawless?

The *qi* of infancy, which is supremely soft is the soft breathing of a baby. Softness is also the supreme attribute of water in the *Laozi*, as we have already seen. And the water-filled *jian* mirror, dark as the deep water of an abyss, which one should make flawless, is the mirror of the mind/heart, which should be still and without a ripple to reflect clearly.

The reason that breath control clears the mind is because an association between one's actual breath (*qi*) and the *qi* of the mind/heart is assumed. By stilling the breath, one stills the mind/heart. Thus, in the *Zhuangzi*:

> Yan Hui said, "May I ask about the purification of the mind/heart?"
> Confucius said, "When you unify your will (*zhi* 志), you do not listen [i.e., understand] with the ears, but listen with the mind/heart. When you do not listen with the mind/heart but listen with *qi*, listening will stop at the ear and the mind/heart stop at what tallies with it. As for *qi*, it is that which being empty, awaits things. Only the way accumulates in emptiness. Emptiness is the purification of the mind/heart." (II *zhong*, 4 *Ren Jian Shi*, p. 147)

Pure *qi*, then, is that which is in the mind/heart when it is empty of all reactions to things.

90

The will (*zhi* 志) may move the mind/heart. When *Zhuangzi* spoke of "unifying" ("making one") the will, he apparently meant that it should not move in any direction. What is actually moved by the will is the *qi* of the mind/heart. Similarly, according to the *Mencius* (IIA.2),

> (Mencius): The will (*zhi*) is the governor of *qi*. *Qi* is what fills the limbs. Wherein the will arrives is wherein the *qi* lodges. Thus it is said, "Hold fast to your will and do not violate your *qi*."

> (Gongsun Chou): Since you have already said " Wherein the will arrives is wherein the *qi* lodges," why do you also say, "Hold fast to your will and do not violate your *qi*"?

> (Mencius) said: When will is stopped up, then it makes *qi* move; when *qi* is blocked up, it makes the will move. . . .

Here, *qi* seems to move in channels, like a stream enclosed within banks.

Mencius (IIA.2) also speaks of nurturing his "flooding (*hao ran* 浩然) *qi*" and when asked what he means, he says:

> It is difficult to explain. This is *qi* which is supremely large and supremely firm. If it is nurtured with straightness and unharmed, then it will fill up the space between heaven and earth. This is *qi* which matches rightness with the way. Without these, it will starve. It is that which accumulated rightness generates. It is not that right [acts] are done again and again and one takes [the principle] from that. If there is no gratification in the heart from one's actions, it will starve.

Mencius' "flooding *qi*," then, must have the mind/heart as its source or it will dry up.

In the *Xunzi*, the concept of *qi* has become closely integrated in a more self-consciously conceived ethical system associated with the rites. In the following passage, Xunzi is discussing people's response to music:

All lascivious sounds beguile people and they respond with unchanneled (*ni* 逆) *qi*. When unchanneled *qi* takes form, disorder is generated therein. Correct sounds beguile people and fluent *qi* responds to it. When fluent *qi* takes form, order is generated therein . . . The gentleman uses bells and drums to guide the will (*zhi* 志) and zithers and lutes to please the mind/heart. . . . Thus, when music is performed, the will is clarified. The rites are cultivated and actions succeed. The ears and eyes are perspicacious and the blood and *qi* are harmonious and peaceful. . . . (20 *Yue Lun*, p. 281)

Here, *qi* is described in terms that we have already seen are associated with the flooding waters controlled by Yu, *ni* 逆—used for water flowing outside its course, and *shun* 順 for water that follows a course. Like water, *qi* runs in channels or else flows uncontrolled outside of them.

Qi in its attenuated mistlike form, on the other hand, moves freely. As the Nameless Man in the *Zhuangzi* (III *xia*, 7 *Ying Di Wang*, p. 294) advised, "Let your mind/heart roam in the flavorless, blend your breath (*qi* 氣) with the featureless and accord with the manner in which living things are so of themselves, not leaving room for self interest, and all under heaven will be in order." Rather than concentrating one's mind/heart and clarifying the *qi*, as in the *Laozi*, or directing the *qi* in channels, the *Zhuangzi* advocates its free movement. In all of these examples, however, *qi* can be understood as modeled on water and water vapor.

The concept of *qi*, then, is modeled on water in all its forms. In the natural world, it is literally the cycle of water that runs down in streams, rises as mist, falls as rain, and gives life to the plants. As human breath, it is that which gives us our vitality. And as the vital energy of the mind/heart, it is that which controls our thoughts and emotions, the sources of our moral sensibilities.

Chapter 4

Sprouts of Virtue

The European, accustomed to thinking of man as a
rational animal and of the mind as a reasoning
instrument, is bewildered by the metaphor of the
seed of grain . . .
—Donald J. Munro, "The Family Network, the
Stream of Water, and the Plant: Picturing
Persons in Sung Confucianism"

Figure 8. View of Stream and Grove,
by Huang Ding, Qing Dynasty (1644–
1911). *National Palace Museum,
Taipei, Taiwan, Republic of China.*

Water is that which gives life to the *wan wu* 萬物, or "myriad living things," as I have been translating this term. According to the *Laozi*, the highest good is like water and what is good about water is that "it benefits the myriad living things." Furthermore water "does not contend and stays in places the multitude detest. Therefore it approximates the Way" (*Dao* 8). The *dao*, too, nourishes the myriad living things: "The *dao* is the watercourse for the myriad living things (*De* 21; 62). And "The *dao*, wending and weaving, can flow left or right. It achieves success and accomplishes its task, but we do not call it 'having.' The myriad living things turn to it, yet do not take it as their ruler" (*Dao* 34). The imagery here is that of the *dao* as an irrigation channel or stream of water which provides nourishment for plants; like water, the ruler who is attuned to the *dao* nourishes his people, but does not claim possession of them.

Water takes so many different forms that its potential for generating imagery is greater than that of other natural phenomena and water is the most powerful metaphor in early Chinese philosophical thinking. As we have seen in the previous chapter, many of the core concepts of Chinese philosophy, including that of the *dao*, are grounded in water metaphor. These concepts were not limited to any particular philosophical school, but shared by Confucians and Daoists—and indeed by other contemporaneous schools that are beyond the scope of the present study. Water's significance, however, did not derive solely from its many permutations. Water is ultimately the source of all life. In this chapter, I shall argue that while early Chinese philosophers meditated on water because they assumed that the principles which informed its many manifestations could be applied to the cosmos as a whole, plant life served as a model for understanding the nature of that which water nourishes, both plant and animal.

Whereas we make a radical distinction between plants and animals, in the Chinese conceptual scheme plants and animals are classified together in a single category, *wu* 物. Because plant growth and regeneration are the focal to the concept of *wu*,[1] the principles of plant growth are extended from plants to an understanding of all living things, including humans. Thus, people are not "reasoning animals" but living things which have a certain potential for growth when they are nurtured properly. As a species, they are defined by the uniqueness of their minds/hearts. Thus it is by fully developing the mind/heart that a person becomes most fully human. The recognition of this metaphor provides the key to understanding the Mencian concept of the goodness of human nature, with its idea of sprouts of goodness in the human mind/heart, as well as Daoist ideas of spontaneity or "being so of oneself."

The Myriad Living Things (Wan Wu 萬物)

The term *wan wu*, which I have been translating as the "myriad" (*wan* 萬, literally, ten thousand) "living things" (*wu* 物) is usually translated as either the myriad or ten thousand "creatures" or the ten thousand "things." The difficulty with the translation "creatures" is that it limits the term to animal life, but "things" in English are primarily inanimate objects. Neither corresponds precisely to the classical Chinese, for *wu* refers to both plants and animals. Here we find a key difference between our own patterns of categorization and that of the ancient Chinese.

I translate *wu* as "living things" because the myriad *wu* are conventionally described as "generated" or "living" (*sheng* 生) and because English has no ordinary expression that includes both animals and plants. However, this translation is also misleading because it sets up an opposition in our minds between living and nonliving things. This opposition is not relevant to the Chinese pattern of categorization since *wu* are not juxtaposed to other things that are dead or inanimate. Furthermore, some things, such as earth and stones, that "change" (*bian* 變), though they are not in our terminology "living," may also be included in the category of *wu* 物.

The character *wu* 物 has a cow signific (牛) and in oracle bone inscriptions it is a color term, something like "brindled" or "mottled" in English, used for multicolored sacrificial animals.[2] In Western Zhou texts, *wu* has a meaning of "variety"[3] and this may be the origin of its usage with reference to the multitudinous "living things" in the world. As we shall see in the following, the *wan wu* include all the living things in the cosmos, of which people are one. However, the prototype for the concept of *wu* as a philosophical category is plant life. People, as a member of this same category are thus likened to plants and the manner in which their life pattern resembles that of plants is stressed.[4]

The *Analects* do not refer to the "ten thousand" living things but the same meaning is expressed with less hyperbole as the "hundred" (*bai* 百) living things. The prototype of this category in the following passage is clearly plant life with its annual cycle rather than animal life:

> The Master said, "I would rather not speak." Zigong said, "If you did not speak, then how could we, your disciples, transmit anything?" The Master said, "Why should the sky/ heaven speak! The four seasons (*shi* 時) proceed therein and the hundred living things are generated (*sheng* 生) thereby. Why should heaven speak!" (XVII.17)

Here, sky/heaven is understood as the natural order and the generation of the living things is identified with the passing of the four seasons. Many animals also have annual cycles of fertility and generation, but plant life is at the root of this concept of the relationship between the season and living things.

Similarly, the *Mencius* (VIA.9) tells us:

> Do not be surprised at his majesty's not being wise. Even among the most easily propogated (*sheng* 生) plants (*wu* 物) in the world, there have never been any which would grow if exposed to one day's heat and ten days' cold. I see the king but rarely. When I retire, the coldness is extreme. What else could happen to the sprouts (*meng* 萌) which are there!

In this passage, *wu* can only be translated as "plant." The effect of Mencius' teaching is like the sun shining on a newly planted sprout—the sprout of virtue that would grow within the mind/

heart of the king if nurtured by the heat of Mencius' teaching.

The association of *wu* with plants is also evident in the following passage from the *Laozi* in which the sage recognizes the full life cycle in their new growth:

> The myriad living things (*wan wu*) arise side by side; I see their return in this. The living things [under the sky/heaven[5]] flourish abundantly and each goes back again to its root. This is called "stillness" (*jing* 靜). Stillness means to return to the natural order (*ming* 命). To return to the natural order is called "constancy" (*chang* 常). (*Dao* 16)

Wu include animals and humans, but the imagery suggests plants that die down to their roots and become still or dormant in winter.

Ming 命—originally "command," as in the "command" or "mandate of Heaven"—is often translated as fate. However, *ming* is not predestination—an idea that comes to China only later with the introduction of Buddhism—but fate in the sense that there is a natural order in which all living things are like plants that germinate, flourish, and then die down. As this passage from the *Laozi* makes clear, *ming* encompasses a continuum of change: that which is "constant" (*chang* 常) is not that which is unchanging, but the regular and constant changes of the natural world. Just as plants can only grow if the seeds are germinated at the right time and given the proper conditions, no "living thing" can only develop fully if it is at odds with the season (*shi* 時). Laozi, on the one hand, stresses that our death is implicit in our birth, our decline in our success. The natural order overrides everything else. To the Confucian, on the other hand, tragedy is when a person of pure virtue and wisdom is born at a time of historical decline.

The *wan wu* may be defined as things which *sheng* 生 or are "*sheng*ed." *Sheng* is often translated as to "live" or "be born." With an object, it becomes transitive, thus to "give birth" or, in A. C. Graham's more sensitive terminology that more easily incorporates plant imagery, to "generate." The earliest character is a pictograph of a plant sprouting from the earth, written Shang Dynasty oracle bone and Zhou bronze inscriptions as:

㞢　㞢　㞢

Like *wu*, *sheng* refers equally to the plant and animal world.

The pattern of naming is significant because when we translate *wan wu* as the myriad creatures that are "born," the imagery of animal birth—which takes place as a discrete dramatic event—reinforces our preconception about an initial beginning. Furthermore, if we regard *sheng* as the generation of new plant life, we are much more aware of the continuum of the reproductive process. Scientifically, this distinction is, of course, dubious, for animals are also born of seed and the Chinese classification of plants and animals together as living things that are generated (*sheng*) is reasonable.

In the Chinese scheme, the norm for all living things is that after they are generated, they flower, and bear fruit before dying. Because they fruit, the species continues. Men too are born, come to maturity, *reproduce* and die. As Confucius tells us, "There are indeed cases of sprouting, but not blossoming! There are indeed cases of blossoming, but not bearing fruit!" (IX.22). But these are the tragic exceptions. Because reproduction is assumed to be a normal—and essential—part of the life pattern, there is a continuum, expressed in the form of the ancestral lineage. And, indeed, the bearing of children is a requirement of the filial son in Confucianism.

According to the *Mencius*, the sky/heaven (*tian* 天) "generated" (*sheng* 生) the people and the myriad living things (IIIA.5, VA.7). In the *Laozi*, the *dao* takes on many of the cosmic aspects of heaven found in the early Confucian texts including the generation of the myriad living things. In the passage from the *Laozi* translated above (*Dao* 16), the dying off of plants when they return to their roots was described as "returning to the natural order (*fu ming* 復命)" and returning to the natural order, as "constancy" (*chang* 常 or *heng* 恒). In the *Laozi*, constancy is the most significant attribute of the *dao*: "The *dao* can be spoken of, but it is not the constant *dao*" (*Dao* 1).[6] From this passage, it is clear that the "constant *dao*" is not constant in the English sense of unchanging, but encompasses a continuum of regular changes in which living things are generated, flower, and "return to their roots."

o is a life-giving force that generates all the living things,
is so in the manner in which water gives life, not in the
of a creator god:

> Regression (*fan* 返) is the movement of the *dao;* weakness
> (*ruo* 弱) is the means of the *dao*. The living things under
> heaven were generated by "something" (*you* 有); "some-
> thing" was generated by 'nothing' (*wu* 無). The *dao* gener-
> ated one; one generated two; two generated three; three
> generated the myriad living things." (*De* 4[7])

The myriad living things that reproduce themselves are part of
a continuum in which things that flower or give birth thereby
begin to die.

Heaven and earth are also *wu*, but they are unlike the
"myriad" *wu* in that they do not reproduce ("generate"] themselves and so they do not, like plants which have flowered, begin
to die: "Heaven is old and the earth is ancient. The reason that
heaven is old and the earth is ancient is that they do not generate themselves (*zisheng* 自生)" (*Dao* 7). Heaven and earth, here,
are not eternal but simply very old. Their peculiarity within the
category of *wu* is that because they do not reproduce themselves,
they change more slowly than other "living" things. On the same
principle, some later Daoists attempted to prolong their life in-
definitely by preserving their seed, refraining entirely from sex
or redirecting their semen so that it does not leave their bodies.

That people, like plants, normally flower and fruit before they
die is, of course, a readily comprehensible metaphor within our
own conceptual scheme. However, it is *not* the *root* metaphor of
our conception of human life. Indeed, as we have seen, the differentiation between plant and animal is so marked in English that
there is no common term which encompasses both. We readily
associate ourselves with animals, but not with plants, and we
regard human life as bounded by the dramatic acts of animal
birth and death. Correspondingly, in religious terms, in the Judeo-
Christian tradition, individuals have lives that were endowed to
them by God. Birth and creation are conceptualized as specific
events and correlated with one another as initial beginnings,

matched by death and, potentially at least, the apocalypse. Individuals are responsible to God for the acts they commit during the time they are alive and each person must answer to God at death.

The traditional Chinese conception, however, is that of an ancestral lineage. During their lifetimes, individuals are exemplars of their lineage. They are not responsible to a transcendent creator for what they do during their lives, but to their ancestors, descendants, and immediate families. They should act as filial children toward their parents during their lives and after their deaths, when they continue to give them food offerings, just as they nurtured them in their old age. The feeling between parent and child, their natural feelings of love and affection, may be extended to others and this is the basis of social morality and of the ideal Confucian state. When people distinguish themselves during their lifetimes, their virtue—*de* 德—is passed down to their descendants and their reputations enhance their ancestors.

Virtue or Inner Power (De 德)

De 德 is something peculiar to people, an aspect of their hearts that other living things do not have. It is conventionally translated as "virtue" in Confucian texts; in Daoist texts, it is sometimes translated as "inner power" or "potency." It is frequently paired with *dao* 道 and it is one of the earliest of all Chinese philosophical concepts. It is also one of the most complex with a range of meanings difficult to comprehend. A. C. Graham, who translated *de* as "potency" in the *Zhuangzi*, noted that it means virtue in the sense that "the virtue of cyanide is to poison," that is, like the Latin root *virtus*, it refers to something intrinsic. Furthermore, *de* "had been traditionally used of the power whether benign or baleful, to move others without exerting physical force. Confucius uses it in this sense of the charisma of Zhou which won it universal allegiance, but moralizes and widens the concept, so that it becomes the capacity to act according to and bring others to the Way."[8] This charismatic power to move others is also an aspect of the Polynesian concept of *mana*, with which the Russian scholar Vassili Kryukov and the Chinese, Qiu Xigui, as well as many earlier scholars, have compared the term.[9]

When *dao* and *de* are paired, the way is understood as the natural course of the myriad living things, the manner in which they are "so of themselves" and *de*, as Graham states, becomes the capacity to act according to the *dao*, "way." Roger Ames has described *de* by stating that "at a fundamental cosmological level, [*de*] denotes the arising of the particular in a process vision of existence. The particular is the unfolding of a *sui generis* focus of potency that embraces and determines conditions within the range and parameters of its particularity. . . ." As we have already seen this "process vision of existence" is the *dao* which is rooted in water imagery. *De* as the "*sui generis* focus of potency" is that which gives people their particular forms.

De was already an important concept in Western Zhou bronze inscriptions which speak of "clarifying the mind/heart and revealing the *de*" (*ming xin zhe de* 明心哲德); thus, we know that the mind/heart was the receptacle of the *de*.[10] These inscriptions also speak of the "perfect *de*" or its "corrective power"(*zheng de* 正德) transmitted to the worshipper from his ancestor, from which we know that *de* was both hereditary and particular to the family or clan.[11] This particularity of *de* distinguishes it from *xing* 性 or "nature" which is also associated with the heart/mind. All people have the mind/heart of a human being and the "nature" or *xing* associated with it, but individuals and their clans or families have different kinds of *de*. If we think of *de* by analogy with plant reproduction, its meaning becomes clearer. Just as all plants (or animals) tend to reproduce according to their own kind, there are different types of plants within a species (red oaks, white oaks, etc.) and some specimens are nevertheless better, stronger, healthier, and more beautiful than others. All people have *de*, and it can always be cultivated to advantage, but some people are born with unusual *de*.

In the *Shuowen, de* 德 is defined as *sheng* 升, "arising." The earliest history of this character is unclear. An oracle bone character sometimes taken as an antecedent is:

However, the meaning of this character and its relationship *de* is uncertain. [12] Another oracle bone character that may be related to *de* in the later script is made up of a sprout (*sheng* 生) growing over an eye:

This character is sometimes transcribed as: 眚 and taken as a phonetic loan for *sheng* 省, to "inspect." Alternatively, it is transcribed as *zhi* 直, "straight."

Although the eye element is written vertically in the modern form of *zhi* 直, it can be identified with the horizontal element of the character *de* 德. When the heart element (心) is added in bronze inscriptions, the character is clearly an antecedent to *de*:

This character is sometimes transcribed as 悳. It has a separate entry in the *Shuowen* dictionary which says "externally it is obtained from others; internally, from oneself," but this definition and its usage in bronze inscriptions suggest that it is an alternative form of *de*, more commonly written with the addition of the movement signific 彳 (occasionally with the foot added to make 辶). Other forms of the character include speech (言) and person (人) significs:

Zhi, as Roger Ames has pointed out, may best be understood "in its more fundamental meaning of "to grow straight without deviation" in the context of organic issuance. The organic dimension of *zhi* is underscored by its cognates, *zhi* 稙, "to sow" and *zhi* 植, "to plant". . . The heart and mind element in this variant character again contributes a sense of disposition to the basic meaning of organic germination and growth."[13]

In Zhou bronze inscriptions, a cowry shell element (*bei* 貝) is commonly substituted for the element above the eye (*sheng* 生?) in this character. In ancient China, as in many cultures across the world, the cowry shell was an emblem of fertility, presumably because it was thought to look like a vagina. In any case, cowry shells had a particular role as sacred objects in the gift-giving of the Western Zhou and were closely associated with the *de* 德 of those who gave them or used them in sacrifice.[14]

In the *Mencius* and other Confucian texts, *de* is a moral term. Moreover, in the *Mencius*, man's moral nature, his impetus toward goodness, is described with the metaphor of "sprouts" growing in the mind/heart, as I will discuss below. Philologically, as Ames has observed, *de* has an association with both plant growth and the mind/heart. Furthermore, we know from those bronze inscriptions that speak of "clarifying the mind/heart and revealing the *de*" that *de* was to be found in the heart/mind. This suggests a conceptual relationship between *de* and the sprouts of goodness; that people are able to be good because of their *de*.

In some contexts, *de* may best be translated as "favor" or "grace." In bronze inscriptions, the ultimate source of this grace which is passed down hereditarily was Shang Di, the lord on high or *tian*, the sky/heaven. This tradition is reflected, for example, in Confucius' statement that, "Sky/heaven generated *de* in me" (*Analects* VII.23). In the textual tradition, *de* continues to be something passed down hereditarily, as it was in the bronze inscriptions; thus, for example, according to the *Mencius*, "The *de* of King Wen only fell into decline after one hundred years" (IIA.1). Furthermore, as Vassili Kryukov and other scholars have observed, *ming* 命, "mandate" or "order" also carries the meaning of "gift" and there is often a correspondance in Western Zhou bronze inscriptions between *de* and *ming*. More precisely, the "perfect *de*" sent down by Shang Di, the Lord on high, or sky/ heaven, to the ancestors from whom the Zhou kings inherited it in early Western Zhou bronze inscriptions was transformed into *tian ming* 天命, the "mandate" or "gift" of sky/heaven.[15]

In the *Mencius*, people's natural inclination toward goodness is continually mowed down, hacked away, or exposed to the coldness of life's vicissitudes. In the *Laozi*, too, we find that *de* in people is at its greatest in the naked baby (*De* 14; 55). In the *Zhuangzi*, *de* is described as that which informs the *wu* 物, the "living thing," that is, the human body, giving it its shape. Thus, there was a man of incredibly hideous appearance to whom both men and women were nevertheless attracted. Even rulers fell under his spell and tried to hand over their states to him. The reason for his ugliness, according to Confucius—in whose mouth *Zhuangzi* is fond of putting his own words—was that his *de* had failed to shape his body. The heart/mind, which is the receptacle of *de,* was like a pond of water:

> Being level is the culmination of water which has come to rest. It can be taken as the standard [for levelness] because it is protected inside and undisturbed outside. As for *de*, it is the cultivation (*xiu* 修) of a complete harmony. *De* which does not take shape [in the physical body], is a matter of the living thing (*wu* 物) not being able to separate. (II *xia*, 5 *De Chong Fu*, pp. 214–15).[16]

De, then, is associated with the mind/heart. It is something with which people begin, and what gives them their physical appearance.

The *Laozi* also describes *de* with reference to water. "The greatest potency (*shang de* 上德) is like a mountain stream" (*De* 3; 41). Water imagery is also suggested in the following passage:

> This is what is called the dark potency (*xuan de* 玄德). The dark potency is deep and distant; it regresses with the living thing (*wu*) and thus reaches the great course. (*De 24*; 65)

The adjective *xuan* "dark" used here for *de* is linked with deep springs as we have already seen. Furthermore, in the passage from the *Xunzi* with which we began this study (28 *You Zuo*, pp. 390–91)—which listed water's various attributes and their ethical equvilents—we were told, "Water which extends everywhere and gives everything life without acting (*wuwei* 無爲) is like virtue (*de* 德)."

De, as we have seen, was a "gift" or "grace"; a fluid compared with a stream that gives life to the myriad things. It is "generated" (*sheng* 生), ultimately from the sky/heaven or the Lord on High and then transmitted hereditarily. It contains the potential of the individual person, both his inner power and his physiognomy, the *de* of one family or clan differentiating it from another.

All these aspects of *de* suggest an association with semen—the water that contains the seed of people. Significantly, because human seed is liquid—a water—the plant and water metaphors coalesce at this point.

The more specific term for semen—and for the female sexual fluids that must combine with it to create offspring, as well as for one's innate vital energy—is *jing* 精.[17] Like *de*, this is also a philosophical term—translatable as "quintessence" or "essence"—and the two are often used interchangeably.[18] However, *de* is also used in the texts as a euphemism for a sexual "favor." The earliest reference that I have found of this usage is in the *Book of Songs* where an unfaithful husband is described as "scattering his *de*" (*er san qi de* 二三其德, *Wei Feng*, 58; see also *Xiao Ya*, 229).

In sum, the concept of *de* can be understood as a quality that is passed on hereditarily within a family. Though a fluid, it is also a seed that gives life. When it develops, becoming "so of itself," it is the full character of a person, an inner power that is also expressed in their physiognomy. *De* is what distinguishes one clan or family from another, as well as each individual within that clan (thus it contains what we would call the genetic makeup). When people have an unusual presence, this is because of the unusual power of their *de*. At the level of root metaphor, the imagery of *de* is based on that of a seed, or, more precisely, water that contains the seed or essence of people. Within this seed is the potential expression of each person's individuality and hereditary characteristics as a member of his lineage.

As a philosophical concept, *de* is an inner vitality, that quality which develops and defines the whole human being. In the Confucian texts, one should "adorn" or "cultivate" (*xiu* 修, e.g. *Analects* VII.3) this vital power. In the *Analects*, the idea of the "son of the lord" (*junzi* 君子) is transformed from an hereditary concept of social class into an ethical ideal. At the same time, the concept of *de* was transformed from an inner power or "mana" which was particularly powerful among those of high social rank into an ethical term. Thus the "adorned inner power" of the man of high hereditary position became the "cultivated virtue" of the Confucian philosopher.

This transformation of meaning is evident in a passage in which Hui, the ruler of the state of Liang asks Mencius what sort of *de* is necessary to be king (i.e., one who rules "all under the sky/heaven"]. The question implies that different people are endowed with different types of *de*. However, Mencius replies that the ruler already has sufficient *de* if he would only use it and goes on to recount a story that someone had told him about the ruler not being able to bear the sight of an ox trembling in fear because it was about to be slaughtered and offered in sacrifice. This example of his compassion was evidence that if he nurtured his *de*, it would be sufficient to rule the world. He need only direct his compassion to people rather than misdirecting it to animals (IA.3).

This *de* of the ruler who could not bear to see an animal suffer is that very same human heart that cannot "bear the suffering of others." And, according to Mencius, this heart is characteristic of humans and evidence that human nature (*xing* 性) is good (IIA.6). *De*, then, was something that people are born with and have the potential to develop. However, it must be adorned and cultivated to become virtue. *Xing* is what is common to all people.

Nature (Xing 性)

Xing 性 is conventionally translated as "human nature." *Xing*—with a heart radical (忄)—and *sheng* 生, which I have been translating as "generate" are commonly acknowledged to be closely related words. Indeed, the two words probably had the same pronunciation and were indistinguishable before *xing* acquired the heart signific. In Zhou bronze inscriptions, *sheng* is used in contexts where *xing* appears in later texts.[19] In the following, I will first discuss Mencius' use of the term *xing*, which is somewhat different from that of Xunzi.

According to *Mencius* (VIIA.1), "To use one's heart to its fullest capacity is to know one's nature (*xing* 性). If one knows one's nature, then one knows the sky/heaven. Preserving one's heart and nourishing one's nature is the means by which one serves the sky/heaven. Regardless of whether one is to be short- or long-lived, one cultivates oneself and waits. This is how one establishes the natural order (*ming* 命)." The same idea was summarized later in the *Doctrine of the Mean* (*Zhong Yong* 中庸 1/1a) as "Sky/heaven's order (*tian ming* 天命) is what is meant by nature (*xing*)." *Ming* or "order" is used here in the same sense in which the *Laozi* used it when he described the myriad living things returning to their roots as *ming*.

Just as *sheng* 生 is usually understood as meaning to "be born" or "live," *xing* 性 is interpreted as that which is "inborn" or "innate" and explained as referring to the qualities with which one is endowed at birth. However, by recognizing that the concrete imagery of *sheng* encompasses plant generation as well as animal birth, we have a clue to the meaning of the abstract concept of *xing*, as it appears in the *Mencius*. Recent scholarship recognizes that *xing* is a dynamic, not a static term.[20] Its dynamic aspects can best be understood if we think of it in terms of a metaphor deriving from the organic world. *Xing*, at least in *Mencius*, is not so much the "qualities that a thing has to start with" (Waley)[21] or even the "sum total of our genetic and individual inheritance" (Roth),[22] but the potential contained by a seed or the first shoots of a seedling to become a fully developed plant.

Xing, as Mencius makes clear to Gaozi, is not a quality like whiteness:

Gaozi said: "What is generated (*sheng* 生) is what is meant by nature (*xing* 性)."

Mencius said: "Is what is generated (*sheng*) being what is meant by nature (*xing*) like what is white being what is meant by white?"

"It is so."

"Is the white of a white feather like the white of white snow? Is the white of white snow like the white of white jade?"

"It is so."

"If it is so, then is the nature (*xing*) of a dog like the nature of an ox and the nature of an ox like the nature of man?" (VIA.3)

Mencius' question is rhetorical and clearly meant to be incontestable: different things—jade, snow, horses—may share the same quality, such as whiteness, but the *xing* or "natures" of a dog, ox, and man are *by definition* different because they belong to different species.

In the following passage, in which Mencius is trying to explain why some men are bad, there is a clear association between the idea of *xing* and species. This passage also demonstrates that the model for the concept of *xing* is found in plant life:

> Mencius said, "It is not the shoots (i.e., original material, *cai* 才) endowed by heaven which are different, but that which ensnares the mind/heart that is so. Take barley: having broadcast the seed, you rake the earth over it. If the earth is the same and the time of planting is also the same, the seed will burst forth and come to life (*sheng*) and when it comes to the summer solstice, [the plants] will all ripen. Should there be differences, they are because of differences in the fertility of the soil, the nourishment of the rain and dew, or the uneven application of human labor. Therefore, all things of the same type (i.e., species, *lei* 類) are alike. Why do you doubt this only in the case of man? The sage is of the same type as we are." (VIA.7)

In a similar vein, Mencius states in another passage that "As for [man's] doing what is not good, this is not the fault of his original material (*cai*) " (VIA.6).

Within the first shoots, there is the potential of a plant even though the shoots have none of the characteristics of the mature plant—no stalk, branches, or leaves—and the sprouts of spring may never bear the fruit of autumn. Every type (*lei*) of living thing, that is, every species, will have its own nature. What distinguishes man's nature (*xing*) from all other living things is his human mind/heart (*xin* 心). Although inheritance is certainly implied, it is the common inheritance of the species, not that of any particular lineage. Furthermore, *xing* encompasses the entire pattern of growth and decline, not only the potential with which one begins—the original material (*cai*). The model includes both the potential to develop in a certain way (what is contained in the seedling) and the characteristics of the mature specimen.

That nature (*xing*) is that which would grow if the first shoots of a plant (or human mind/heart) were nurtured and allowed to develop into fully mature plants is also evident in Mencius' famous description of Ox Mountain:

> The woods of Ox Mountain were once beautiful, but since they are on the outskirts of a great city, the woodchoppers have hewn them; can they still be regarded as beautiful? It is not that sprouts and shoots do not grow (*sheng*) there when the mountain, having been given a respite in the evening, they are moistened by rain and dew. But the oxen and sheep come and graze on them once again; that is why it is so barren. When people see how barren the mountain is, they think of it as never having had tree shoots (*cai* 材) on it. How could this be the mountain's nature? How, of what exists in people, could there not be a mind/heart with a sense of humaneness (*ren* 仁) and right and wrong (*yi* 義). The manner in which their good mind/hearts are lost is like the case of the woodchoppers in the woods. Since every morning [their good mind/hearts] are hewn down, can they still be regarded as beautiful? If people's likes and dislikes are scarcely similar to other people when they have had the respite of the evening and the vapor (*qi* 氣) of the early dawn, then it is because of what they did during the course of the day. If their revival is disturbed again and again, then the night vapor (*qi*) will be insufficient to preserve them. If the night vapor is insufficient to preserve them, then the distance which separates them from the birds and beasts is not long. When people see how beastly they are, they consider that they never had the original material ("shoots," *cai* 才) [of goodness] within them. How could this be the essence (*qing* 情) of human beings? Hence, there is no living thing (*wu* 物) that will not grow if it is nurtured; but if it fails to be nurtured, there is no living thing which will not expire. (VIA.8)

Here, the shoots of timber on Ox Mountain are equated with

the potential of people's mind/hearts for goodness. Like plants, which have an innate tendency to grow and are fed even by the evening moisture but cannot withstand continually being hewn down, the mind/heart has an innate tendency to be good that will try to reassert itself, but eventually be overcome by outside pressure.

The "Shoots" (*Cai* 才, 材)
(Original Material or Natural Endowment)

In the Ox Mountain story from the *Mencius*, the *cai* 才, which contains the natural endowment and latent potential for goodness in the human heart is equated with the *cai* 材 of the forest. On a literal level *cai* 才 is the seedling or first shoots of a plant; the addition of the tree radical 木 makes it more specific but the two characters *cai* 材 and *cai* 才 are often interchanged. *Cai* means timber or wood as a raw material, and it has similar etymological origins to the English word "matter," which also refers to wood. The wood of "matter," however, as Graham pointed out, is cut up and ready for the carpenter. *Cai*, however, is grounded in the image of a seedling. It is the first shoots of the trees in a forest rather than wood as matter, an inanimate substance already prepared for the carpenter.

In the *Zhuangzi* (II *zhong*, 4 *Ren Jian Shi*, pp. 170–72), as well as the *Mencius*, the *cai* of a tree is compared with that of a man:

> When Carpenter Shi reached Quyuan on his way to Qi, he saw a chestnut-leaved tree used as an altar of soil. Its size was so great that it shaded several thousand oxen and it measured a hundred span in girth. Its height approached that of a mountain and it was seventy feet before it had branches. Over ten of its side-shoots were large enough to make a boat. The people gazing at it were like a market throng, but the carpenter did not glance over his shoulder and continued traveling without halt.
>
> When his apprentice had gazed to his fill, he ran to catch up with Carpenter Shi and said, "Since I took up axes and followed you as my master, I have never seen timber (*cai*

:autiful as this. Why is it that you aren't willing to
l travel on without halting?"

:arpenter] said, "Enough, don't say any more! It's
lousy wood. If you make boats from it, it will sink; if you
make coffins of it, they will rot right away; if you make
vessels, they will decay quickly; if you make door leaves,
they will drip sap; if you make a pillar, it will be wormy.
This is a tree which does not have any potential (*cai* 材). It
has nothing that can be used. Thus, it is able to be long-
lived like this."

When Carpenter Shi had returned home, the chestnut-
leaved altar of earth appeared in his dream and said, "What
would you compare with me? Would you compare me with
hardwood trees, the sorts of trees which have fruit and
berries—the cherry-apple, pear, orange, and pomelo? When
their fruit is ripe, they are stripped. When they are stripped,
they are abused: the large branches are broken off and the
small ones ooze. This is a case of their ability [to be used]
making their life miserable. Thus, they do not live out their
natural (*tian* 天) years, but meet misfortune in midcourse.
They are things which customarily cause themselves injury.
There are no living things (*wu* 物) which are not like this.
Moreover, I have been seeking to not have any potential
use for a long time; and now, when I am approaching death,
I have obtained it. For me, it is of great advantage. Supposing I did have a use, would I have had the chance to get this
big? Moreover, you and I are both living things (*wu*) and
how could living things know one another? And how could
a no-good man who is approaching death know about a no-
good tree?

Mencius argued that all people have sufficient potential, *cai*, to
grow into a good and humane persons. But *cai*, like quality of
timber, can differ from person to person. Conventionally, everyone wants to have great native ability. Zhuangzi, on the other
hand, argues here that for a person, as for a tree, lack of capa-
bility—uselessness—is of more value than wasting one's life in
being used. All living things, all *wu*, have *cai* and all will die in

the end, but those without use to the world are more likely to live out their natural life span.

In the story of Uglyface Tuo, both men and women were inevitably attracted to him even though his *de* 德 had failed to shape his body because his "*cai* 才 was whole" though his *de* 德 "virtue" had failed to shape his body. When asked what he meant by *cai* being whole, "Confucius" replied:

> Death and generation, preservation and perishing, failure and success, poverty and riches, worthiness and unworthiness, blame and praise, hunger, thirst, cold and warmth—all such changes are due to the movement of the natural order (*ming* 命). They alternate before us day and night, but intelligence cannot calculate their beginnings. Thus, they are insufficient to disturb our harmony and not to be admitted to the spiritual storehouse [*ling fu* 靈府, i.e., the mind/heart]. Make [the mind/heart] harmonious and happy, communicative but not lost in pleasure; ensure that night and day without gap, it acts as springtime to the living things. This is someone who, whatever he encounters, generates the appropriate season (*sheng shi* 生時) within his mind/heart. (*Zhuangzi*, II *xia*, 5 *De Chong Fu*, p. 212)

For the *cai* to be whole then, is for the potential—the shoots within the heart—to maintain their vitality so that they respond to life as a plant responds to springtime. It is this meeting of the mind/heart with one's time that creates a sense of harmony.

The Sprouts (*Duan* 端) of the Mind/Heart

According to Mencius, what separates people from the birds and beasts and defines their nature is their mind/heart (*xin* 心) which must be nurtured. This is because the mind/heart contains emergent shoots (*duan* 端) that sprout to become goodness. These sprouts are what make people human:

> This is why what are called men all have a heart which cannot bear the suffering of others. Now, supposing some-

one suddenly sees a child about to enter a well, everyone will have a mind/heart of pity and compassion. It is not because they wish to ingratiate themselves with the parents of the child; it is not because they want to be praised by their fellow villagers and friends; it is not that they do so because they cannot stand [to hear] its cry. From this we can see that to be without a mind/heart of compassion is not to be human. To be without a mind/heart which feels shame is not to be human. To be without a mind/heart which yields [to others, e.g., elders] is not human. To be without a mind/heart which discriminates right and wrong is not human. When the mind/heart which feels compassion, it is [because of the] sprout (*duan* 端) of humaneness (*ren* 仁). When the mind/heart feels shame, it is the sprout of the sense of right and wrong (*yi* 義). When the mind/heart yields to others, it is the sprout of ritual propriety (*li* 禮). When the mind/heart discriminates right and wrong, it is the sprout of wisdom (*zhi* 智). These four sprouts which people possess are like their having four limbs. To have these four sprouts and deny one's own ability is self-mutilation. To deny the ability of one's ruler is mutilation of the ruler. (*Mencius* IIA.6)

Duan 端 means a tip or point or, more abstractly, a beginning or an end. As the commentators to the *Mencius* have pointed out, its meaning in this passage is that of an earlier form of the character that did not have the 立 (standing) signific: 耑. When the character first appears (in the late Zhou Dynasty), it is written as:

耑

According to the *Shuowen,* it is "the tip of a living thing (*wu* 物) when it is first generated (*sheng* 生)," that is, the head of a child when it is first born, or the emergent shoot of a plant when it first sprouts; hence the meanings of the tip or point or beginning associated with the character *duan*. Graphically, according to the *Shuowen,* the upper part resembles something growing (*sheng* 生); the lower part resembles a root."

Humaneness (Ren 仁)

The mind/heart which feels compassion when the child is about to fall into a well is one of *ren* 仁, "humaneness" or, as it is often translated, "benevolence." In the *Mencius*, it is this feeling of compassion and its consequent expression in "humaneness" which must be cultivated by the ruler if he wishes to become a true king to whom all the people in the world will turn.

In the *Shuowen*, *ren* 仁 is defined as *ren ye* 人也, "human." According to the *Mencius*, "Humaneness (*ren* 仁) is the human mind/heart (*ren xin* 人心)" (VIA.11) and "One who is humane (仁) is human" (VIIB.16). More precisely, taking the analogy of the plant, "humaneness" is what will develop when the nodes in the heart sprout and are allowed to grow. It is this peculiarity of the heart that defines people as human, and differentiates them from animals with whom they share the bestial desires for sex, food, and so on. This is a person's distinctive feature and so it is his "nature" (*xing* 性). "Humaneness," then, is to be human in the fullest sense, the state that people reach when the shoots which sprout in their hearts have been nurtured to attain their greatest glory. To be "humane" (*ren*) is to be the most perfectly developed example of the human species.

That which Is So of Itself (Ziran 自然)

Daoist sages do not cultivate the sprouts in their mind/hearts—nor hack them away. By "doing nothing" (*wuwei* 無爲), they allow things to be "so of themselves" (*ziran* 自然). *Ran* 然 is a very general verb that means to "be so." As such, it is a common verb indicating assent: "it is so," "it is like that"—or in the negative, "it is not so." *Zi* is a reflexive pronoun. It means "self" and was originally a picture of a nose, to which the Chinese still point to indicate themselves in the same way that we point to our heart. Thus (following A. C. Graham) *ziran* may be translated as to "be so of oneself." It is also commonly translated as "spontaneous" or, as a noun, "spontaneity," "natural" or "nature," the meaning which it still carries in modern Chinese.

Just as the *dao* (like water) does nothing, but benefits the myriad living things, those living things are "so of themselves," that is, they develop their full potential, spontaneously, just as watered shoots become full-grown plants. Both *wuwei* 無爲, "doing nothing" and *ziran* 自然, "being so of oneself," occur as descriptions of water and of the *dao*. According to the *Zhuangzi* (VII *xia*, 21 *Tian Zi Fang*[23], p. 716). "When water comes bubbling up [as a spring], though nothing is done, it is so of itself (*ziran*)." The *Laozi* also tells us that the *dao* "takes as a model that which is so of itself" (*Dao* 25).

The *Laozi* and the *Zhuangzi* are both concerned with the principles which govern the organic world in general rather than the specific nature of man. The *Laozi* does not caution us against taking pride in the happenstance of being born human, as the *Zhuangzi* does, but it does continually make the point that we are but one of the myriad living things. The sage king must intuitively grasp the rhythms of the natural world and refrain from contrived policy if he is to rule successfully, or even survive— just as the butcher in *Zhuangzi*'s famous story understands the anatomy of a carcass so well that he carves it without ever meeting resistance, finding the joint so perfectly every time that he never needs to sharpen his knife.

Wei 爲, "deliberate action" is, as we have already seen, the peculiarity of human beings and it prevents things being "so of themselves" (*ziran* 自然). The butcher who perfectly understands the carcass acts, that is, he carves, but he does so without deliberation and with such intuitive knowledge that his knife is never dulled. As the Nameless Man in the *Zhuangzi* (III *xia*, 7 *Ying Di Wang*, p. 294) advised, "Let your mind/heart roam in the flavorless, blend your breath (*qi* 氣) with the featureless and accord with the manner in which living things are so of themselves, not leaving room for self interest, and all under heaven will be in order."

If the ruler, like water, does nothing, then people will "be so of themselves," or "transform themselves" (*zihua* 自化). Still water will become clear of itself and moving water will bring benefit to the myriad living things without willing to do so. Similarly, the people will transform themselves in response to the virtue of a sage ruler. According to the *Laozi* :

> The *dao* is constant and nameless (alternatively: does not act and nothing is not done).[24] If the lords and kings can keep to it, the myriad living things will transform of themselves (*zi hua* 自化). (*Dao* 37)

Similarly—and here the water metaphor is particularly clear:

> I do nothing and yet the people are transformed of themselves.
> I am fond of stillness (*jing* 靜) and the people correct themselves (自正). (*De* 16; 57)

Hua 化, which I translate here as "transform," means change. It is used for the metamorphosis of, for example, cocoons into butterflies, and refers in Daoist texts to all the transformations of the life cycle in the organic world, from birth or generation to death. If the ruler, like water, does not "act" then he will be "still," and the people will be nourished and reflect his clarity in their behavior.

The Artificial and the Natural (*Wei* 僞 and *Xing* 性)

Mencius argued that one must nurture the sprouts in one's mind/ heart so that they will develop fully. These are the moral qualities which distinguish a man as such, which make a human (*ren* 人) humane (*ren* 仁). Although the moral qualities have to be nurtured, like sprouts, they cannot be assisted in their growth. Thus, he argued against Gaozi's assertion that rightness is external by stating:

> Your mind/heart must not forget [rightness], nor assist its growth. Do not be like the man from Song. In Song, there was a man who was worried about his sprouts not growing

117

and pulled on them. Exhausted, he returned home and told his family, "I'm worn out today! I've been helping the sprouts grow." His son rushed out to see the sprouts, but they had already withered. The people in the world who do not "help the sprouts grow" are few; those who consider this as useless and refrain from it are the people who do not [even] weed the sprouts. Those who pull on the sprouts are people who would help them to grow, [but] this is not only useless, it also harms them. (IIA.2)

The sprouts of the mind/heart—the senses of humaneness and right and wrong—must be nurtured (weeded and watered), but they cannot be manipulated; nor, as we have seen of the tree shoots nibbled by sheep on Ox Mountain, can they survive if they are continually destroyed. In Daoist terminology, they must be allowed to be "so of themselves" (*ziran* 自然).

Elsewhere in the *Mencius* (VIA.1), nature (*xing*) is equated with the willow tree as opposed to the cup that may be made from its wood. Once again, the metaphor is established by Gaozi, but not disputed by Mencius:

> Gaozi said: "Nature is like the willow tree. Rightness (*yi* 義) is like the bowls. To regard human nature as humane and having a sense of right and wrong is like taking the willow tree as the bowl.

> Mencius said: "Are you able to make bowls by following the nature of the willow? Or do you first hack and mutilate the willow and make bowls from it afterwards? If having hacked and mutilated willow, you would make bowls from it, then to make people humane and give them a sense of right and wrong, you would hack and mutilate them, would you not? Your theory is surely one which would lead everyone to demolish humaneness and rightness!

In this passage, as in the one about the man of Song who sought to help the sprouts grow, Mencius is concerned not simply with defining human nature, but with governing. To control the people, one must cultivate the sprouts in their mind/hearts, which

118

make them tend toward goodness. They may be led by following their nature, just as one would follow the grain of wood to carve a bowl, but going against their grain will only destroy the goodness which is inherent in them.

As many other scholars have noted, there is a fundamental difference in definition in Xunzi's argument with Mencius about whether human nature is good. Mencius, on the one hand, understood *xing* 性, "nature" as the nature of the species, that which distinguishes man from animals. Thus, he was able to demonstrate that Gaozi did not understand human nature by showing that Gaozi's argument resulted in an equation between the "nature" of humans and the "nature" of dogs or oxen. In the *Xunzi*, on the other hand, *xing*, "nature" is not human nature as opposed to that of other species, but that which one does naturally as opposed to *wei* 偽 "artifice," that is, it is deliberate human action or skill:

> Human nature is bad. As for [human] goodness, this is a matter of artifice (*wei*). Now, as for human nature (*xing* 性), when man is born (*sheng* 生), there is the love of advantage in him. He follows this; therefore contention is generated and the courtesy in which one yields to others declines. When he is born, there is dislike and envy in him. He follows these; therefore violent theft arises and loyalty and good faith decline. When he is born, there is the love of music and female beauty in the desires of his eyes and ears. He follows these; therefore promiscuity and disorder are generated and ceremonial behavior, a sense of right and wrong, culture and principles decline. (*Xing E Pian* 23, p. 327)

In this exposition, the selfish desires with which one is born are "human nature" (*xing*). These are desires people share with animals rather than something that distinguishes the human from the beast. Thus, the definition of *xing* has changed from what distinguishes humans as a species to what the human being would do naturally. In the *Xunzi*, the moral virtues, the learned artificial behavior that sages have created, not their nature, are what distinguishes the human from the animal.

Wei 偽, which I have translated here as "artifice" has a man (*ren* 人) added as a significic to *wei* 為. *Wei* 為, as a noun, means deliberate action, as in the expression *wuwei* 無為, "without action." The man radical marks the *Xunzi*'s specialized usage of the term *wei*, but there is no phonetic or semantic distinction between the two characters 為 and 偽. Thus, the addition of the man radical to the character may be regarded simply as an attempt to mark a particular nominal usage rather than as a representation of a different word. Here, then, we have a common language of discussion with the Daoists but a philosophical disagreement. The *Laozi*, on the one hand, would have us refrain from actions and "do nothing" (*wuwei* 無為). The *Xunzi*, on the other hand—in opposing Mencius' definition of human nature as good—defines these "actions" as the very criteria for civilized or "human" behavior.

In the *Xunzi*, this artifice or "doing" is not only necessary but the unique contribution of the ancient sages, the means to direct people's mind/hearts and make the world ordered and humane. The *Laozi* argues that we should return to the natural state that existed before the sages created the ideas of virtue, humaneness, and rectitude. This natural state, before the interference of the sages with their artificial values, is called *pu* 樸, conventionally translated as the "uncarved block." This term is closely related to *cai* 材 (or 才), a shoot or seedling, encompassing the ideas of raw material and potential. The translation "uncarved block" is meant to suggest wood that has not been adorned by an artisan. The imagery of unworked timber is certainly focal to its meaning. According to the *Laozi*, "When the *pu* (timber) is split apart, it becomes vessels, when the sages are employed, they become the chiefs of the officials" (*Dao* 28). Nevertheless, the translation "uncarved block" suggests wood that is already prepared and entirely inanimate, whereas *pu* is a natural state more like unworked timber than an uncarved block. It is a tree or branch that has not yet been subject to human manipulation. Similarly, *pu* 璞 written with a jade rather than a wood significic, refers to the crude, encrusted rock which contains jade (or, usually, nephrite in ancient China).

Pu is a state to which we can still return if we maintain our constant *de* 德 or "virtue." As this same passage has already told us: "Be a river valley to the world and your constant virtue will be sufficient. When your constant virtue is sufficient, then you will move toward (*gui* 歸) a natural state (*pu*)." As we have already seen, "constancy" is not to be unchanging, but encompasses the seasonal patterns of time.

Chapter 5 ────────────

The Philosophers

> Water is the blood and *qi*-breath of the earth; it
> resembles what courses through the veins and
> arteries. So, it is said that water is the potential
> for everything.
> —*Guanzi*, Chapter 9 "Water and Earth"

Figure 9. Discussing Antiquity by the River, by Dong Qichang, Ming Dynasty (1366–1644). *National Palace Museum, Taipei, Taiwan, Republic of China.*

In the previous chapters, we have seen that many of the most fundamental concepts of early Chinese philosophy are grounded in the imagery of water and the plant life that water nourishes. In this chapter, we will look at the manner in which individual philosophers (or, more properly, philosophical texts) used these concepts to develop particular philosophical systems. As we have already seen, the concepts had a range of possible meanings and particular philosophers extended or varied these meanings according to their own purposes, but the manner in which they did so was guided by the inherent potential of the concrete imagery on which the concepts were modeled. For example, the concept of *dao* 道 is grounded in the metaphor of a waterway. It may refer to a course of behavior, but when its range of meaning is extended to include that order which prevails throughout the world when all people behave as they should, then the imagery extends to a system of rivers flowing within their proper courses; and when the concept encompasses an idea akin to what we call time, the root image is that of the water itself, shapeless and invisible.

The range of meaning of any particular concept and its potential for development should accord with its original concrete model. However, this is not an absolute rule because once the concept is established it can develop independently of the inital model and other images may also be used as metaphors to develop its meaning in a different manner. Nevertheless, since the imagery is inherent in the concept, it will inevitably influence the manner in which people think with it. *Dao*, for example, had become an abstract concept long before the period in which our texts were written; so the manner in which this concept was extended is probably not attributable to a conscious awareness of its metaphoric roots, but to the inherent implications of an abstract concept originally modeled on water.

The philosophical ideas modeled on water and plant life form a network of interlocking meaning. For example, *qi* 氣 ("vital energy") and *dao* 道 ("way") are not isolated ideas and their conceptual relationship reflects their common roots in water imagery. Thus, the concept of *dao* is modeled on a waterway and by extension water in its various forms. *Qi* takes water vapor as its model, but its extended meanings also suggest water in its other forms, from hardened ice, to moving water, to dissipating vapor. In humans, *qi* is both breath and vital spirit. In the physical world, it is the mist which is transformed into rain and the water of the streams, that which gives life to the myriad living things; on an abstract level, it is the component of the *dao*. Significantly, this concept crosses what we perceive—but the Chinese did not— as a boundary between the physical and the transcendent by tying the person, as a physical creature to the larger cosmos, both to the physical world in which *qi* is mist and to the immaterial cosmos in which *qi* is vital spirit.

The concept of the *xin* 心 or "mind/heart"—the organ of thought, desire and emotion—was also modeled on water. The *xin* is like a pond; it is clear and reflective when still, but able to move along a certain course when directed to do so by the will. Thus, the Confucian ruler, on the one hand, who governed as a true king, directed his mind/heart along the way of humane government. He nurtured his "virtue" or "potency," so that it nourished the mind/hearts of the people, like water nourishes plant life. As a consequence, the people turned their hearts to him and gave him their allegiance. The Daoist sage who "did nothing" (*wuwei* 無為), on the other hand, did not channel his will like the Confucian, but let it course freely along the way, nevertheless nourishing all that it came upon.

Water is essential for life. All living things are nurtured by it and agriculture depends on it. In classical Chinese, the "myriad living things" (*wan wu* 萬物) include people, as well as plants and animals, the concepts of *de* ("virtue" or seed) and *cai* ("potential" or shoots), are modeled on plant life that may flourish or decline, according to the season and in response to the water that it may or may not receive. Plants have an obvious seasonal pattern of generation, blooming, reproduction (dropping seed), and dying (or dying down) and this pattern is also extended to human society. On the one hand, people exist within an ancestral lineage, rather than as individuals before a transcendent god, just as plants are part of a continuum of generation and reproduction. On the other, they are dependent on the seasonality or timeliness of their efforts to succeed in the world, just as a

126

plants can only survive if they are set out in the appropriate season.

The mind/heart is like a pond, but—according to Mencius at least—it also has "sprouts" within it. These account for people's tendency to goodness if they are nurtured by a good ruler under whom the way prevails. Since these sprouts are only found in people and not in any other creature, Mencius defined human "nature" as the possession of these sprouts which are unique to people and described *ren* 仁 "humaneness" as their natural tendency. Although other philosophical schools may not accept Mencius' argument that people are characterized by these "sprouts" of goodness within their mind/hearts, they nevertheless understand people as having a natural endowment (*cai* 才, 材) which is modeled on plant imagery—the newly emergent shoots of a plant—and *de* 德, "virtue" or "potency," which must be cultivated, like seed, or at least allowed to be "so of itself" without interference.

These and the other ideas that I have discussed in the course of this work formed the conceptual scheme from which early Chinese philosophers formulated their ideas. If we think in metaphor or in ideas grounded in metaphor, then our thought is at least to some extent structured by the concrete imagery of that metaphor. This should be reflected not only in the semantic relationships of one concept to another, but in the manner in which the thinkers themselves build their personal systems using these concepts. In conclusion, then, I will briefly analyze the manner in which these concepts function with relation to one another in the philosophical systems of particular philosophers.

My focus will be on the *Mencius* and the *Laozi*, as these two texts have relatively coherent philosophical systems. We shall see that the philosophical systems reflected in these two texts, although radically different and generally understood as opposed to one another, are nevertheless grounded in the same root metaphor, that is, both philosophers think in concepts that are modeled on images of water and plant life and this is reflected in their philosophical systems. Although I will be primarily concerned with the *Mencius* and the *Laozi*, I will discuss the *Analects* as background to the ideas developed in the *Mencius*. The form of the Inner Chapters of the *Zhuangzi*—its earliest section—is frequently anecdotal, and so it makes less use of abstract language than the *Laozi*, but I will also discuss it briefly. Most important, the model of the *dao* as the water which flows within a stream rather than simply the course of the stream is developed extensively in the *Zhuangzi*; therefore, I will use it to demonstrate the range of potential implicit in this concept which is so central to the development of later philosophical systems.

The Analects

The later tradition that Confucius studied water as a means of understanding both the physical cosmos and the principles of human behavior is, as we have already seen, first found in the *Analects* where we were told that Confucius meditated on rivers and water. This tradition is indicative of Confucius' primacy among the philosophers, but we need not suppose that interest in water was original to him. The concept of the "way," *dao* 道, for example, which was central to Confucius' philosophy (as it was to all later Chinese thought) was already grounded in the metaphor of water flowing spontaneously within a channel or course.

In the *Analects*, there are many "ways" or "courses." The "way" may be that of the sky/heaven, of the good king, or of the gentleman—that which flows inevitably from his position. Or more generally, the *dao* is the sum of all those courses, those patterns of movement and behavior that are inherent in an orderly cosmos. Thus, the world—*tianxia* 天下, that below the sky/heaven—may "have the way," or it may be without it, when there is no one following the way of a king. In the *Analects*, we also found the first use of the term *wuwei* 無爲, "doing nothing." "One who governed without acting (*wuwei*) was Shun. Why act! He simply assumed a respectful demeanour and faced south" (XV.5). In return, the people "turned their mind/hearts toward him" (*gui* 歸) (XX.1). The ancient kings did not need to act; they simply followed the way of a king (like water moving within its course).

Two of the major concerns of the *Analects* are familiar ones: the definition of the good man and the problem of why a good man may not succeed in the world. In Confucius' time, theoretical speculation about human nature and the mind/heart had not yet begun. According to his disciple Zi Gong, there were no records that he discussed either the way of the sky/heaven or human nature (V.13), although elsewhere in the *Analects*, we are told that he declared "[People's] natures (*xing* 性) are close to one another, but their practices are far apart" (XVII.2). This passage suggests that although human nature was not yet a subject of philosophical discussion, people's natures—their *xing*—were nevertheless understood as something that people have in common. People's *xing*, "natures" were distinguished from their practice—what they actually do; that is, however similar people may be to start with, we know that they act differently.

The good man in the *Analects* was called a *junzi* 君子,—"gentleman." Confucius described himself as a transmitter, not an originator (VII.1), but here, as in much else, he gave traditional forms new dimensions. To Confucius, a *junzi* was not the son of a lord, but someone who follows the course appropriate to such a position. A gentleman was someone who had set his mind/heart along the way, who cultivated his *de* 德 or potency and behaved according to the rites (*li* 禮). Whereas *xing* 性 corresponded roughly to species, *de* was hereditary and might be passed down within a clan. Although everyone had *de*, some, such as Confucius himself who proclaimed that his *de* was generated by sky/heaven (*Analects* VII.23), were particularly endowed.

A person who cultivated his *de*, a *junzi* was *ren* 仁 "benevolent" or "humane." To be *ren* 仁, humane, was simply to be a *ren* 人, a person in the fullest sense. Humaneness was pursued for its own sake—for there were no supernatural sanctions, no heavens and hells that rewarded or punished after death before the introduction of Buddhism several hundred years later. People were one of the hundred living things and this was the supreme expression of being human. If a ruler could be truly humane, he would act as a father and mother to his people and they would "go to him" as children to a parent, that is, he would be following the course of the true king and so rule over the world.

Confucius declared that neither he nor the sky/heaven need speak because "The four seasons (*shi* 時) proceed therein and the hundred living things are generated thereby. . . ." (XVII.17). Here, the sky/heaven governs the natural order and the generation of the living things which are identified with the passing of the four seasons. The "living things," as we have already seen, include plants, animals and people and sky/heaven governed the seasonality or timeliness that determined the success or failure of human actions, as well as that of the other living things. But, just as a plant, however good the seed, cannot thrive out of season, so too a person cannot flower when the times are unfavorable. Tragedy in this scheme—and it was the tragedy of Confucius' own life—was not a matter of predestination, or being subject to the whims of a willful god, like Jehovah in the Old Testament, but one of being born out of season.

Confucius was ultimately unsuccessful in seeking a ruler to serve because the time or "season" (*shi* 時) was not auspicious for the generation of a new dynasty, just as plants set out in the winter could not thrive. However great his virtue—the *de* 德 or "inner power" that the sky/heaven had generated in him (VII.23)—his activities could not meet with success unless the "season" was right. Thus, he cried, "Oh! The sky/heaven destroys me! The sky/heaven destroys me!" (XI.9) Indeed, Confucius knew that the season was inauspicious to establish a new dynasty because of the absence of the appropriate physical omens in the natural world: "The phoenix does not arrive. The river does not give forth a diagram. I am finished, aren't I?" (IX.9). The diagram or "plan" (*tu* 圖) here refers to a diagram that the Luo River gave forth in the time of the great Yu, who dug out the river channels and arranged the nine provinces.

The Mencius

Mencius' development of the earlier Zhou theory of *tian ming* 天命, the "mandate" or "order" of sky/heaven, and his argument that human nature is good are generally regarded as his most important contributions to the development of early Chinese thought. If we now look at the relationship between these two ideas in the light of their underlying imagery of water and plant life, we can see that these two theories form part of a single philosophical system grounded in the root metaphor of water and the plant life it nourishes.

Let us first look at Mencius' concept of *tian ming*. Here we find development of the idea of seasonality expressed in the *Analects*. As in the *Analects*, *tian* 天, sky/heaven, is the supreme arbiter, that which governs both the movements of the heavenly bodies that mark what we call the passage of time and the seasons on earth. The idea of seasonality was already present in the *Analects*, but is developed further by Mencius. According to the *Mencius*, a change of dynasty should occur about every five hundred years and the "time" or "season" of a new dynasty was already overdue in his own time. Although there still seems to be some possibility that *tian* might act wantonly in the *Analects*, *tian* has become an abstraction which awards its "mandate" (*ming*) automatically, according to a natural order in the *Mencius*. This order is an ethical one, but it is modeled on the same cosmic principles which govern water and plant life. The king who enacts humane government allowing the way to prevail in the world is like the water which makes plants grow; and the mind/hearts of the people who turn to him are like well-watered plants.

Mencius does not use the term *wuwei* 無為, but he does tell us that given the "nature of that below sky/heaven" (*tianxia zhi xing* 天下之性), the wise ruler does not "bore through" things, but follows the example of the flood hero Yu, who knew better than to attempt to bore through mountains: "if knowledgeable men were like Yu in directing the water, then there would be no dislike of knowledge. Yu's means of moving water was to make it move where it had no resistance (*xing qi suo wu shi* 行其所無事). If knowledgeable men would also make [people] move where there was no resistance, then their knowledge would be great indeed!" Furthermore, Mencius goes on to explain, the sage understands the past instances (*gu* 故—this term can refer to astronomical as well as historical phenomenon). Thus, he can effortlessly benefit the people, just as the astronomer could calculate the movement of the heavenly bodies without moving from his seat (IVB.26). Similarly, one should not be like the man of Song who tried to help the seedlings grow by pulling at them (IIA.2).

Although the mind/hearts of the people respond to the humaneness of a good ruler like sprouts watered by timely rain, their movement away from an oppressive king to a good one is also like the movement of water which flows in channels and goes downward; that is, the ruler is like both timely rain and the great river or sea to which all tributaries lead, and the people (whose mind/hearts are modeled on both water and plants) like sprouts which spring up when well-watered and the tributary streams which flow into larger bodies of water. The term used to describe the people who move from a bad ruler to a good one, *gui* 歸, connotes the movement of a tributary to a larger river or stream, as we have already seen.

Mencius specifically denies that the sage rulers of the predynastic period might have abdicated their rule or that the founders of the first dynasties had to fight to overthrow the evil kings of the previous dynasties. Pestles could not have "swam in blood" when King Wu of the Zhou Dynasty defeated the last king of the Shang Dynasty, because the "most humane smote the most inhumane" (VIIB.3). Instead the people simply went from one ruler to the other, a natural, indeed an unpreventable process, like water flowing downward.

In the predynastic period, the people turned from the evil son of the good ruler to his successor; in the dynastic period, from the bad last king to the founder of the new dynasty.[1] Jie and Zhou were the legendary last kings of the Xia and Shang Dynasties, archetypes of evil rulers. They received the rule by heredity, but lost the mind/hearts of the people and therefore their rule:

That Jie and Zhou lost the world was that they lost their people. Losing their people was losing their mind/hearts. For obtaining the world there is a way (*dao*): if you obtain its people, you have got the world. For getting its people there is a way (*dao*): if you get their hearts, you have the people. For getting their mind/hearts there is a way (*dao*): accumulate for them what they desire; do not foist on them what they hate. People turn to (*gui*) humaneness (*ren*) like water flowing down and animals running to the wilds. Hence, what causes fish to flee to the deep spring is the otter. What makes a sparrow flee to a thicket is a kite. What made the people flee to Tang and Wu [founding kings of the Shang and Zhou Dynasties] were Jie and Zhou. Now, supposing there was one among the rulers in the world who liked humaneness, then the feudal lords would all cause the [people] to flee to him. Even if he did not desire to be king, he would not be able to get [his wish]. Those who wish to be king nowadays are like people who having [already] had an illness for seven years, seek three year old artemesia. If they do not nurture it, they will not get it in their lifetime. If one does not set one's mind/heart on humaneness, one will have anxieties and disgrace for one's whole life and thereby sink into death and destruction. (*Mencius* IVA.9).

Thus, the people turning toward humaneness is inevitable. The ruler need only set his mind/heart on humaneness; though he does not desire to be king (i.e., he need not *do* anything, to obtain it), he will nevertheless *be* the person to whom all the people's minds and hearts will turn.

In another passage, Mencius was asked who might give the rule (*yu* 與). This is probably, as D. C. Lau has pointed out, a reference to the abdication legends of the predynastic period. Mencius replied by declaring that people will give their allegiance to a humane king naturally, just as sprouts respond to rainwater:

Your majesty knows about seedlings—if there is a drought in the seventh and eighth months, then the seedlings wither up. If the sky/heaven becomes ponderous with clouds and suddenly pours rain, then the seedlings spring up revived. Who can prevent it being so? Now, as for the shepherds of the world, there has not yet been one who is not avid to kill people. If there was one who was not keen on killing people, then the people of the world would all crane their necks, looking forward in expectation to him. If he were truly like this, the people would turn to (*gui* 歸) him, like water pouring down so copiously, how could anyone restrain them! (IA.6)

This process—the people turning from an oppressive ruler to good king—is what is meant by a change in the "mandate of heaven." *Tian ming* 天命—which I have translated as the "natural order" in the *Laozi* can also be understood in that sense here, that is, the "mandate of heaven" is a natural order, not a personal command.

Mencius' cosmos is a moral one. There is *dao* under the sky/heaven, when there is a ruler who follows its mandate. Sky/heaven controls the seasons, both those of the natural world and those of human society. The true king follows the way of the sky/heaven, and establishes a lineage which will inevitably decline. The people respond to the humane ruler because their mind/hearts respond to goodness. As a species, people are uniquely endowed by sky/heaven (or, as we would say, by nature) with mind/hearts which gives them the potential (*cai* 才) for goodness. This potential consists of "sprouts" (*duan* 端) in their mind/hearts which, when nourished, will make them humane, understand right from wrong, behave with propriety, and be wise, as we have already seen in the previous chapter. This potential—these sprouts—respond to the good ruler who in turn nourishes them with humane and just rule, just as plants respond to water. Like the sprouts on Ox Mountain, cut to the quick by grazing sheep, people's mind/hearts can be stunted by oppressive conditions. Nevertheless, people will still respond to good rule, flourish, and develop into moral human beings.

The *ming* of the sky/heaven is thus a natural order and a new dynasty is established when the *dao* prevails in "that below the sky/heaven," that is, when there is a good king who exercizes humane government so that the people turn to him, like the rivers which flow inexorably to the sea. A person fulfils the natural order by fulfilling his potential as a moral being, his "nature," which consists of the sprouts (*duan* 端) within his heart:

A gentleman desires extensive territory and numerous people, but that in which he finds joy does not lie therein.

A gentleman finds joy in standing at the center of the world and making the people within the four seas settled, but that which he takes as his nature (*xing* 性) does not lie therein. What a gentleman takes as his nature is not increased if he exercizes great power, nor decreased if he dwells in poverty. These are a consequence of his lot [in life] being settled. What a gentleman takes as his nature are humaneness, a sense of right and wrong, and wisdom; these are rooted (*gen* 根) in his mind/heart. They appear in his face's serenity, give form to his back and extend to his four limbs. The four limbs do not speak but they illustrate [the goodness of his mind/heart]. (VIIA.21)

All men have this potential for goodness, and all are endowed by the sky/heaven with the inner power or virtue of *de* 德, but those who cultivate this seed grow into unusual specimens of humankind. Their distinction marks their features and is manifest in their bearing just as a well nourished plant looks healthy. A person who so develops this uniquely human virtue to its fullest extent is *ren* 仁, "humane."

Individuals, as well as that under sky/heaven, have *ming* 命. And just as the natural order of the cosmos is a moral one, so too is the natural order of an individual human life: "To use one's mind/heart to its fullest capacity is to know one's nature (*xing*). If one knows one's nature, then one knows the sky/heaven. Preserving one's mind/heart and nourishing one's nature is the means by which one serves sky/heaven. Regardless of whether one is to be short- or long-lived, one cultivates oneself and waits. This is how one fulfils the natural order (*ming* 命)" (*Mencius* VIIA.1).

Ming is often translated as "fate," but with its connotations of predestination, the translation, once again, erroneously projects ideas from a transcendent scheme upon the Chinese immanent worldview. A person's *ming* is not what is predestined, but one's moral potential:

Mencius said: "There is nothing which is not natural order (*ming* 命). If one follows along with it (*shun* 順), one receives its full measure. This is why one who knows the natural order does not stand beneath a crumbling wall. To die, having fulfilled the course of one's life, is to have the full measure of the natural order. To die, withered and shriveled, is not to have the full measure of the natural order." (VIIA.2)

The terms that I have translated here as "withered and shriveled" (桎梏) normally connote the dying off of plants. As John Knoblock has pointed out, *tian ming* in the *Xunzi* is often best translated "the natural order."[2] Here we see that *tian ming* in the *Mencius* is also the natural order, though, in the *Mencius* that order includes the sprouts of goodness that are found in the human mind/heart.

The Laozi Daodejing

The *Laozi* is roughly contemporaneous with the *Mencius*, but it was not only written in opposition to the Confucian school, it was written for a different audience and with a different aim than the *Mencius*. Mencius wished to find a ruler whom he could assist in unifying the world "under sky/heaven." He assumed that the cosmos was morally ordered and he sought to discover and formulate the principles that could assist in bringing about the foundation a new dynasty and the unification of the known world. He wrote for the would-be king and when Confucianism became the orthodoxy of imperial China, his theories of the mandate of heaven and the goodness of human nature served as the ethical grounding of the state and were the means for judging the legitimacy of particular rulers and dynasties.

The *Mencius* provided the moral standards by means of which Chinese society judged itself in later history. The *Laozi*, on the other hand, was written for the ruler of a small state, or even for the individual, who in a time of political chaos wished primarily to survive. Laozi rejected the Confucian idea of a morally ordered cosmos: "The sky/heaven is not humane (*ren* 仁)" (*Dao* 5). And condemned the values of philosophers such as the Confucians and Mohists whose theories, he believed, were responsible for the decline of society from a state of primeval perfection: "Eliminate the sages and get rid of the wise men and the people will benefit a hundred fold. Eliminate humaneness and get rid of the principle of right and wrong and the people will recover filial and parental love. Eliminate craft and get rid of profit and their will be no thieves and muggers." (*Dao* 18). Indeed, it was these very values that led to the parlous state of the present world: "So, the great way is disregarded and therein are humaneness and the principle of right and wrong. Wisdom and compassion emerge and therein is great falsehood" (*Dao* 18).

Unlike other early Chinese philosophers, Laozi was totally unconcerned with the ancient sage kings so important to the Confucians and the patterns of history that these kings were believed to exemplify, that is, with timeliness (*shi* 時) and the mandate of heaven. Nevertheless, the root metaphor of Laozi's philosophical system was the same as that of the *Mencius*—water and the plant life that it generates. In the *Laozi*, the *dao* takes precedence over *tian*, the sky/heaven, as a first principle. Here, the imagery of the *dao* is extended from the waterway to the water itself with all its manifold properties. Thus, for example, the way is described in language that is also appropriate to water: "insipid; tasteless. Looking at it, it cannot be seen. Listen, and it cannot be heard. [But] when you use it, it cannot be exhausted" (*Dao* 35).

The *Laozi*'s advice to the ruler or person who would survive in perilous times and ultimately overcome was, quite simply, to imitate the attributes of water. Water nourishes all the living things and they all turn to it, but it does not lord its power over them:

> The *dao*, wending and weaving, can flow left or right.
> It achieves success and accomplishes its task, but we do not call it "having."
> The myriad living things turn to it (*gui*), yet do not take it as their ruler.
> The myriad things turning to someone, but not taking him as their lord, can be called being great. For this reason, the sage's ability to achieve greatness is because he does not act great. Hence, he is able to achieve greatness. (*Dao* 34)

In other words, the sage ruler or official should be like water in nourishing his people. He should be indifferent to his position and the people—like the other myriad things—will live naturally, simply, and without the adornments of craftsmen or the theories of wise men, with their bellies full and their mind/hearts empty of extraneous and misleading ideas.

One effect of this shift from the supremacy of *tian*, the sky/heaven which governs timeliness, to the *dao* and the redefinition of the *dao* from the waterway to the water itself is a loss of moral imperatives. There is no longer any particular way which one should follow. The *Laozi* advocates the imitation of water, but this is simply a strategic tactic. Water is soft and weak and it does not contend, yielding to the hard and strong and descending to the lower position, but it ultimately overcomes. It "does nothing," but it is nevertheless victorious and nourishes the myriad living things. These attributes, as we have seen, are also those of the way, the *dao*, which is compared directly with water. And they are the personal attributes which the ruler or official or soldier should cultivate because they are both good tactics and, ultimately, of benefit to all.

Not to contend, but to yield before any strong onslaught is the best strategy in life and warfare, just as water does not contend and descends to the lowest possible point:

> Water's goodness is that it benefits the myriad living things (*li wan wu* 利萬物), yet does not contend and stays in places the multitude detest. . . .[3] It is because it does not contend that it is without misfortune. (*Dao* 8)

Not contending and "doing nothing" are two aspects of the same attribute:

> The sage is without action (*wuwei*) and therefore without defeat (*De* 23; 64);

> because he does not contend, there is no one able to contend with him. (*De* 25; 66)

Like Yu, who made the water flow where it was without resistance in the *Mencius*, the good warrior of the *Laozi* avoids a fight:

> One who is good as a knight is not belligerent. One who is good at battle is not roused to anger. One who is good at overcoming an enemy does not confront him. One who is good at making use of others lowers himself before them. This is what is meant by the virtue (or potency—*de*) of not contending (*bu zheng*), what is meant by the power (*li* 力) of making use of others. (*De* 29; 68)

The virtue of not contending is, of course, the primary rule of Chinese martial arts, as well as the principles of warfare in such military texts as the *Sunzi* where the army is advised to retreat in the face of pressure and penetrate any weakness.

Water that does not contend is "soft" (*ruo*) and "weak" (*rou*) and has no will: it "does nothing." So too, the true sage (unlike the Confucian scholar) promulgates no learned theories and "does nothing":

> There is nothing softer and weaker in the world than water; and yet in attacking the hard and strong, there is nothing which can take precedence over it. This is because there is nothing which can take its place. There is no one in the world who does not know that the weakness of water can overcome the strong and its softness, the hard; and yet there are none who can put this into practice. . . ." (*De* 39; 78)

Doing nothing includes wordless teaching by the example of one's inner power rather than promulgating a theory:

> The sage dwells in affairs which are doing nothing and carries out wordless teaching. (*Dao* 2)

> Wordless teaching and the benefit of doing nothing—these are things rarely achieved in the world. (*De* 5; 43)

Thus, by wordless teaching, as by "doing nothing," the sage benefits people, like water benefits the myriad living things.

Softness and weakness are attributes not only of water, but also of young plants and children, and of life as opposed to death:

> When people are born they are soft and weak; when they die they are hard and strong [from rigor mortis]. When the myriad living things, the trees and herbaceous plants are engendered, they are soft and flexible; when they die they are withered and brittle. So it is said: Hardness and weakness are companions of death; softness, weakness, minuteness and fineness, the companions to life. That is why when the arms are strong, one does not win. When the wood is strong, it will be broken. Hence, the strong and great dwell below; the soft and weak, high up. (*De* 37; 76)

Here, the soft and weak dwell high up because they have assumed authority over people who exercised false strength. The terms "softness" and "weakness" used here for young life (as opposed to the old and dead) also suggest a correspondence of youth with "soft," "weak" water.

Water that is still, becomes clear and perfectly level—a moral standard as we have already seen. Here, although the sage promulgates no theories and does nothing, he is still, clear (pure) and perfectly even. By simply being himself, he can act as a standard that can rectify the world.

> Be clear (*qing* 清) and still (*jing* 靜) and you will be able to act as the rectifier (*zheng* 正) of the world. (*De* 6; 45)

Stillness is also another aspect of "doing nothing," the means by which both water and ruler allow things to be "so of themselves":

> When I do nothing (*wuwei*), the people are transformed by themselves. When I am fond of stillness (*jing*), the people act correctly by themselves. When I do not have official duties, the people are enriched by themselves. When I desire not to desire, the people are simple of themselves." (*De* 16; 57)

Just as water "does nothing" and the myriad living things grow, the ruler does nothing, and the people transform themselves; and just as stillness is the means by which water clarifies itself and becomes level, it is also that by which the people become pure and unsullied.

Stillness (*jing* 靜) is also a description of plants which die off in winter, regressing to the "natural order" (*ming* 命). The *Laozi* was not concerned with historical "seasonality" or "timeliness" (*tian shi* 天時) or with the progress of the mandate of heaven, with *tian ming* 天命 as an historical pattern of dynastic rise and fall. In this text, *tian ming* is a natural order and people are but one of the myriad living things. Like all living things, from the moment that they begin to grow, their dying away is already implied. This is something that the sage realizes:

> The myriad living things (*wan wu*) arise side by side; in this, I see their return. The living things [under the sky/heaven] flourish abundantly and each again returns to its root. This is called "stillness" (*jing* 靜). Stillness means to return to the natural order (*ming* 命). To return to the natural order is called "constancy" (*chang* 常). (*Dao 16*)

Thus, water (and the *dao*), which the sage should imitate, benefits the myriad living things. These things, including humans, are subject to a natural order. Dying off is already implied by the growth of new shoots. This is the "constant" way. The ideal is a society governed simply, in accordance with the annual agricultural patterns, everyone living out his natural life span and fulfilling his *ming* 命, without strife or striving to accomplish more.

I have argued that the reason for the correlation between water and plant life with principles of human behavior was an assumption that the same principles inform all aspects of the cosmos. In the *Laozi*, we see attributes associated with water extended into other spheres of life. Thus, for example, soft and weak, which are attributes of water, are also the attributes of young living things, both plant and animal; so water and young life may be correlated as soft and weak as opposed to stones and dead things; and both water and young living things are ultimately stronger than their opposites. That the principles governing water could be applied to human life in this manner must have seemed proof of the water's explanatory power. Indeed, the *Laozi* is marked by a fondness for correlating binary pairs with attributes such as soft and hard, weak and strong, flexible and rigid, descending and ascending, and so forth.

The terms *yin* 陰 and *yang* 陽 are used only once in the *Laozi*, but the pairs which the *Laozi* correlates correspond to the pattern of binary categories later classified under the *yin/yang* rubric. These pairs were complementary, not exclusive, each requiring the other. Originally *yin* and *yang* referred to shady valleys and sunny mountain sides, that is, to topographical features. How *yin* and *yang* came to be chosen as the technical terms that signify the dual nature of the cosmos is not yet clear. Male and female, for example, are a much more common pair in the *Laozi*. Nevertheless, the decision to take topography as the root metaphor for a concept of dualism which was used to classify all of the dualistic aspects of life, society, and the cosmos is a further indication of the centrality of rivers and mountains in the Chinese conceptual scheme.[4]

Proof of the validity of the correlative system was undoubtedly found in its explanatory power. Thus, for example, the female has a remarkable correspondence to water and both water and the female were classified as *yin* in the later theory. Both women and water are soft (*rou* 柔) and weak (*ruo* 弱). They both take the low position. Women are described as "dark" (*xuan* 玄), as is the abyss of the mountain pool. In opposition to men, women are still (*jing* 靜) and "do nothing" (*wuwei* 無爲). All of these attributes of water and the female are taken as superior to their opposites in the *Laozi*.

We are also told that "the living things under heaven were generated by 'something' (*you* 有); 'something' was generated by 'nothing' (*wu* 無)" (*De* 4; 40). This suggests that the system of correspondence extended to male and female sexual organs. Correspondences between categories such as water, the superior sexual strength of the female, "nothingness" or "having nothing" (*wu* 無), and the soft and yielding, versus male sexual weakness, "having something" (*you* 有), and the hard and firm, served as a further confirmation of the explanatory power of the correlative system.

In the *Laozi*, these attributes of water, which are simultaneously those of the female are those the sage should take as his model if he is to survive:

> The female always overcomes the male by means of stillness (*jing*). It is because of her stillness, that it is appropriate for her to take the position below. Therefore, a large state takes over a small state by taking the lower position and a small state, by taking the lower position, is taken by a large state. (*De* 20; 61)

> The reason that the River and the sea rule over the hundred valley streams is that they are good at taking a lower position to them. This is why they are able to be king over the hundred valley streams. This is why the sage who wishes to be in authority over the people always humbles himself in his speech. (*De* 27, 66)

> Know the masculine, but keep the feminine and act as a runnel for [anything in] the world. Act as a runnel to the world and the constant potency (*heng de*) will not depart and you will return again to [a state of] infancy. Know the pure, but keep to the polluted and act as the river valley of that below the sky/heaven. (*Dao* 28)

In these passages, the female is like water in her stillness, lowness, and, indeed, in her pollution, also a characteristic of water which collects detritus when it is "downstream." She does not contend; she "does nothing," but eventually overcomes the male, who "does something," and exhausts himself with his exertions. Thus, like water, she is superior. And both water and the female exemplify a principle that the sage would be wise to follow.

The Zhuangzi

Whereas the *Mencius* was intended as advice for the ruler who would unify all under the sky/heaven and for those who wished to advise such a ruler; the *Laozi* appears to have been written for the ruler of a small state who wishes to preserve himself and the powerless official. The sage who follows the teachings of the *Zhuangzi*, however, rejects official life entirely. In Confucian philosophy, the greatest tragedy for the individual was to be born at the wrong time. However great his inner power (*de* 德) and his efforts, he could not flourish and achieve the potential with which he was endowed in such a time, just as a sprout planted in the winter cold will not thrive. In the *Laozi*, we were told that the end of everything is already evident in its beginning; like plants, people inevitably begin to die off as soon as they have flowered. This theme is even more extensively developed in the *Zhuangzi*, which takes the acceptance of mortality and death—the universal dilemma that is the provenance of many religious traditions—as its primary theme.

As A. C. Graham has observed, the *Zhuangzi* shares two traditional Chinese assumptions: "(1) the generation of things from the ultimate root is not an event at the beginning of time but a continuing process; and (2) the substantial condenses out of and dissolves into the insubstantial."[5] The root metaphor for the first assumption is, of course, plant life and it is expressed in the idea of *ming* 命, the "natural order"; for the second, water as expressed in the concept of *qi* 氣. And both are expressions of the *dao* 道. I have already observed that there is no word in classical Chinese equivalent to the English "time" and that the concept of *ming*, the "natural order" includes the regular pattern of changes modeled on the seasons. The *dao* includes water that flows from a constant source and may be used to discuss what we consider the passage of time (*shi* 逝). Water is also amorphous and transparent and the *Zhuangzi* extends the concept of *dao* by means of this imagery to explore something very similar to what we call "time" as an abstraction.

The individual, according to the *Zhuangzi*, must simply accept that he is but one of the myriad living things. These things may have short lives like the insect who is born and dies within a single day, or they may last as long as Pengzu who lived for five hundred years, but all living things have their spring and autumn, however long their life span. One may prolong life with uselessness, like the tree with its worthless timber, but personal liberation lies in the recognition that people are no different than anything else, subject to a seasonal pattern (*ming*) nourished by a continuous flux (*dao*). "Death and life are the natural order; that they have the regularity (*chang* 常) of night and day is due to sky/heaven" (III *shang*, 6 *Da Zong Shi*, p. 241). And:

> Death and generation, preservation and perishing, failure and success, poverty and riches, worthiness and unworthiness, blame and praise, hunger, thirst, cold and warmth— all such changes are due to the movement of the natural order (*ming* 命) (II *xia*, 5 *De Chong Fu*, p. 212).

Indeed, of the myriad living things we who "having happened specifically to take on human form are even pleased because of it. As for the human form, when it has undergone ten thousand changes, it has not yet begun to reach its limit" (III *shang*, 6 *Da Zong Shi*, pp. 243–44)

One of the most famous stories in the *Zhuangzi* is that in which Zhuangzi whose wife had just died was found drumming on a pot and singing. Charged with shameful insensitivity, he responded that at first he was at a loss, but then he realized that:

> She began and yet at the source she had no life. Not only did she have no life, but at the source, she had no form. Not only did she have no form, at the source, she had no vitality. When mingled in the amorphous, something changed and there was vital energy (*qi*). The vital energy changed and there was form. The form changed and there was life. Now, once again, it has changed and there is death. This is moving together with the four seasons, spring, autumn, winter, and summer. When her person was about to lie down to sleep in the great mansion, I proceeded to sob and wail about it. I myself recognized that I did not comprehend the natural order (*ming*), and so I stopped." (VI *xia*, 18 *Zhi le*, pp. 614–45)

This story is not from the earliest section of the text which is attributable to Zhuangzi himself, but the same theme is found there in a story in which Confucius sends one of his disciples to assist in the funeral of one of three Daoist sages, only to find the other two making music and singing. The sages who comprehend the natural order are freed from concern about death by their recognition that people, like other living things, are simply part of the natural order. This is *ming*. And even beyond *ming*, there is the *dao*. Here the amorphous aspects of water are taken as the model for the "way." The sage who roams with the way, wanders freely without concern for the passage of time and mortality. He not only accepts the pattern of change implied by the natural order, he lets his mind/heart roam untrammeled in the flavorless undifferentiated vastness that is the way. He forgets himself in the way, just as the fish forget themselves in water, returning to a state of absolute emptiness like that before his "ancestor first emerged." He lets his "mind/heart roam in the flavorless, blends [his] breath (*qi* 氣) with the featureless and accords with the manner in which living things are so of themselves, not leaving room for self interest, and all under heaven will be in order" (III *xia*, 7 *Ying Di Wang*, p. 289, 294).

The way is a course, ever passing, but when someone merges himself with it, he is unaware of differences and untroubled by death and mortality. The recognition that the way as a concept is modeled on water is also the key to understanding another of *Zhuangzi*'s major themes: the futility of trying to distinguish "what is" from "what is not." If the *dao* is like water, an undifferentiated flux, then our attempt to make distinctions is but a mirage: "What is 'this' is also 'other' and what is 'other' is also 'this.' They say "That is it; that is not" from their point of view; we say "That is it; that is not" from our point of view. Are there really 'this' and the 'other'?" (I *xia*, 2 *Qi Wu Lun*, p. 66). And the differentions are of our own making: "What is allowable [in argument] is allowable; what is not allowable is not allowable. As for the way (*dao*), one moves along it and it is formed; as for the things (*wu*), one speaks of them and they are so" (p. 67).

Conclusion

The philosophical systems of the *Analects*, *Mencius*, *Laozi*, and *Zhuangzi* which are grounded in the root metaphor of water and plant life place humans entirely within a natural world and holistic system. The distinction between things that are made by human endeavor and those that simply happen according to the natural changes and principles of the universe is first made in the *Laozi* and the *Zhuangzi*. The *Zhuangzi* sometimes uses technological imagery such as potting and bronze casting in a positive manner, but both of these texts privilege the natural as opposed to the human-made.

A clear distinction between the natural and artificial is first made in the *Xunzi*, which draws on the Daoist texts, but regards virtuous behavior as an artificial construct of the sages. This represents an intellectual breakthrough in that it allows the system grounded on the root metaphor of water and plant life to be juxtaposed to another construct and this has important consequences for the development of Chinese thought. The *Xunzi* also represents another stage of Chinese thought as the first text which syncretizes earlier systems. Thus, although I have referred to it herein, any detailed analysis goes beyond the limitations of the present study.

Another trend in the late Warring States and early Han, besides that of syncretism, was the systematization of correlative systems. I have already noted that the binary pairs in the *Laozi* were later categorized under the rubrics of *yin* and *yang* and that *yin* and *yang* originally referred to the topography of mountains and valleys. In the late Warring States Period, water, which was *yin,* as opposed to fire, which was *yang,* became part of a conscious correlative system that was used in various spheres of thought, such as medicine and divination. Water was also one of the five elements in another correlative system based on the number five (*wu xing* 五行), which also became current in the late period and continued to influence later Chinese thought.

In *wu xing* ("five element" or, as alternative translations would have it, "five phase" or "five process") theory, water is one of five correlative categories that also include fire, earth, metal, and wood. These five categories correspond to five colors, musical tones, directions, flavors, and so on. In this theory, the five are normally given equal status, but in an unusual and intriguing text, the "Water and Earth" chapter of the *Guanzi* (39), water is given supremacy among the five elements and described as the source of all life.[6]

The *Analects*, *Mencius*, *Laozi*, and *Zhuangzi*, which I have discussed herein, were core texts in the development of Chinese thought. Anyone acquainted with later Chinese philosophy or aesthetics will, I believe, recognize that the imagery and concepts which I have discussed herein continued to inform Chinese thought. This included not only philosophy per se, but literature, art and all spheres of aesthetics. Other systems intermingled with and influenced the scheme I have described. The earlier systems were syncretized and correlative schemes were used to systematize earlier patterns. Buddhist thought and Buddhist imagery imported from India, which also used water imagery in important ways, mingled with the native Chinese conceptual scheme, adding to its complexity. Nevertheless, the systems which I have described represent a root metaphor for Chinese thought not only of the ancient period but throughout the ages.

Notes

Chapter 1

1. Penguin, 1970, pp. 130–31. I have converted Lau's romanization of the Chinese name to Pinyin, the official system used in mainland China, in order to conform to the usage that I will maintain throughout this work.

2. I owe this suggestion to Christoph Harbsmeier (personal communication).

3. This argument has been most strongly developed by David Hall and Roger Ames. See especially *Thinking Through Confucius* (New York: State University of New York Press, 1987), pp. 12–17. See also Sarah Allan, "Shang Foundations of Modern Chinese Folk Religion," in S. Allan and Alvin P. Cohen, eds., *Legend, Lore and Religion in China: Essays in Honor of Wolfram Eberhard on His Seventieth Birthday* (San Francisco: CMC, 1981), pp. 1–21.

4. D.C. Lau, *Chinese Classics: Tao Te Ching* (Hong Kong: Chinese University of Hong Kong Press, 1989), p. 129, p. 141.

5. Traditionally, the *Laozi* was divided into two sections, the *Daojing* and the *Dejing*, with eighty-one divisions. In the transmitted versions of the text, the *Daojing* precedes the *Dejing* and it is also known as the *Daodejing*. In the Mawangdui manuscripts, however, the *Dejing* comes first and there are no subdivisions. The number divisions that I use in my citations are those of the *Dejing* and *Daojing*, as assigned by Xu Fandeng, 徐梵澄, *Laozi Yijie* 老子臆解 (Beijing: Zhonghua

shuju, 1988) followed by the number of the traditional order where this is different.

6. Xunzi's dates are from John Knoblock, *Xunzi: A Translation and Study of the Complete Works*, see vol. 1 (1988), pp. 3–35.

7. George Lakoff and Mark Johnson, *Metaphors We Live By* (Chicago: University of Chicago Press, 1980), pp. 3, 18, 22. See also George Lakoff, *Women, Fire, and Dangerous Things: What Categories Reveal about the Mind* (Chicago, University of Chicago Press, 1987), for discussion of the relationship of metaphor and the imaginative capacity of thought.

8. G.J. Whitrow, *Time in History* (Oxford: Oxford University Press, 1988) pp. 128–29. This view was not, of course, original to Newton.

9. See p. 37 for a discussion of the terminology in this passage.

10. See S. Allan, *The Shape of the Turtle*, especially Chapters 2 and 3.

11. Donald J. Munro, "The Family Network, the Stream of Water, and the Plant: Picturing Persons in Sung Confucianism" in Donald J. Munro ed., *Individualism and Holism:Studies in Confucian and Taoist Values* (Ann Arbor: Center for Chinese Studies, University of Michigan, 1985), p. 278.

12. Graham was specifically concerned here with opposing Donald Davidson, "On the Very Idea of a Conceptual Scheme" [reprinted in D. Davidson, *Inquiries into Truth and Interpretation*. Oxford: Clarendon Press, 1984, pp. 183–98], but he observes that other philosophical discussions of conceptual schemes almost always make the same assumption. See Stephen C. Pepper, *World Hypotheses: A Study in Evidence* (Berkeley, California: University of California Press, 1970 (originally published in 1942), for an example of the assumption that root metaphors and conceptual schemes are logical propositions.

13. A.C. Graham. "Conceptual Schemes and Linguistic Relativism in Relation to Chinese" as reprinted in A. C. Graham, *Unreason within Reason: Essays on the Outskirts of Rationality* (LaSalle, Illinois: Open Court, 1992), p. 61.

14. See Tao Wang, *Colour Symbolism in late Shang China*, Ph.D. dissertation, School of Oriental and African Studies, University of London, 1993, for the development of color terms in ancient China; Brent Berlin and Paul Kay, *Basic Color Terms: Their Universality and Evo-*

lution (Berkeley, University of California, 1969); and Eleanor Rosch, "The Structure of Colour Space in Naming and Memory for Two Languages," *Cognitive Psychology* III, pp. 337–54. See also, Mark Lakoff, *Women, Fire and Other Dangerous Things* for a summary of the development of color theory.

15. For discussion of the relationship between grammar and logic in ancient Chinese philosophy, see Chad Hansen, "Chinese Language, Chinese Philosophy and 'Truth'," *Journal of Asian Studies* XLIV, no. 3 (May 1985), pp. 491–520.

16. "The Mencian Conception of *Jen Hsing*: Does It Mean Human Nature?" In Henry Rosemont, Jr., ed., *Chinese Texts and Philosophical Contexts* (La Salle, Illinois: Open Court, 1991), p. 147.

17. "The Continuity of Being: Chinese Visions of Nature." In J. Baird Callicott and Roger T. Ames, ed., *Nature in Asian Traditions of Thought* (Albany: State University of New York, 1989), pp. 67–78.

18. *Intellectual Foundations of China* (New York: Albert Knopf, 1989), p. 25.

19. See Sarah Allan, "Shang Foundations of Modern Chinese Folk Religion" and *The Shape of the Turtle*, pp. 19–21, for a fuller discussion of the structural consequences of Chinese religion.

20. See Shima Kunio 島邦南, *Inkyo bokuji kenkyū* 殷墟卜辭研究 (Hirosaki: Chūgokugaku Kenkyūkai, 1971), pp. 188–216; Robert Eno, "Was There a High God *Ti* in Shang Religion," *Early China* 15 (1990), pp. 1–26.

21. See Chapter 5; S. Allan, "The Conceptual Implications of *tian* 天 as Sky," in *Festshcrift* in honor of Léon Vandermeersch, Jacques Gernet and Marc Kalinowski, eds., forthcoming.

22. The Chinese text of the *Analects* cited herein is Yang Bojun 楊伯峻, ed., *Lunyu Yizhu* 論語譯注 (Beijing: Zhonghua Shuju, 1980).

23. Page references for the *Xunzi* refer to *Xunzi Jianshi* 荀子簡釋, Liang Qixiong, ed. (Hong Kong: Zhonghua Shuju, 1974). For Chinese texts cited hereafter, see pp. 166–66.

24. I discuss this term in detail on pp. 79–84.

25. I have followed the traditional (Wang Bi) text here, rather than the Mawangdui manuscripts. For further discussion of this passage, see p. 74.

Chapter 2

1. The oracle bone inscriptions represent a fully developed writing system. Clearly there was a much longer earlier development, but only scattered evidence is yet available. See Nicholas Postgate, Tao Wang and Toby Wilkinson, "The evidence for early writing: Utilitarian or ceremonial," *Antiquity* LXIX, no. 264 (Sept. 1995), pp. 459–80, esp. pp. 467–68.

2. *Shui* has the same form in the simplified characters now used in mainland China and the more traditional complex characters. However, by "modern script" I mean the complex, not the simplified characters of mainland China.

3. V *zhong*, 13 *Tian Dao*, p. 457. For the edition of the *Zhuangzi* and other Chinese texts cited herein, see p. 169.

4. The *Shuowen* says 往也; the *Guangya*, 行也.

5. *Shijing Jizhu*, p. 22; cf., *Shijing* 256.6 (p.161) in which *shi* is used figuratively for words which defame and "cannot be made to pass away" (*yan bu ke shi* 言不可逝).

6. to be distinguished from *shi* 逝, discussed above. Unless otherwise noted, the pronunciations given herein are those of modern Mandarin. This language includes a great many homonyms that are written with different characters and have unrelated meanings.

7. *Han Shu* 32, p. 27–26.

8. The Mawangdui version is 筮, a character with the same sound which means to divine, but the following line which refers to going far away suggests that the received versions are correct after all. The emendation that I make here is also made by D. C. Lau and the *Laozi Yijie*, see p. 35.

9. Various accounts of the flood myth are discussed in *The Shape of the Turtle*, see esp. pp. 67–71.

10. Almost all of the received versions of the text have *bu zheng* 不爭 here and I have followed this tradition. The Mawangdui manuscripts have *you zheng* 有爭. This is variously interpreted. *You* may be a mistake for the negative *bu* 不. *Zheng* 爭 might also be read as *jing* 靜, "still," another common attribute of water (see *Laozi Yijie*, p. 10). Although D. C. Lau argues that it can be read sensibly as "vies to dwell in the place detested by the multitude," the last line which refers again

to "not contending" suggests that a simple mistake in the earlier line is the most likely explanation. For other passages that mention "not contending," see *De* 2; 66 (discussed above), and *De* 33; 68.

11. See *The Shape of the Turtle*, pp. 99–101.

12. See especially *Mozi Jiangu* VIII, 31 *Ming Gui, xia*.

13. Hexagram 49 (*Ge* 革), cf. Hexagram 63 (*Jiji* 既濟 —when water is above fire it disperses) and 64 (*Weiji* 未濟 when fire is above water it disperses). *Zhou Yi Quan Jie*, pp. 343, 440, 448.

14. For early manifestations of this dualism, see S. Allan, *The Shape of the Turtle*, e.g. pp. 37, 67, 70. In that work, I speculated that the application of fire to the plastrons of water turtles to make oracle-bone cracks in Shang divination might be a manifestation of this dualism (p. 111). Since then I have discovered that the *Guanzi* makes this explicit: "Turtles are born in water and one burns them with fire. For this reason, they act as a predicator of the myriad living things and as a determiner of bad and good fortune (XIV *Shui Di*, 39, pp. 4–5).

15. *Xunzi* 9 *Wang Zhi*; 17 *Tian Lun*; 19 *Li Lun*.

16. I take 槐 here as 塊.

Chapter 3

1. *Tao*, the spelling best known to English readers, is the Wade-Giles transcription of this word. The transcription for Chinese that I use herein is the Pinyin system now used in mainland China.

2. *Analects*, p. 11

3. A. C. Graham, *Disputers of the Tao*, p. 22

4. Herbert Fingarette, *Confucius: The Secular as Sacred*, New York: Harper and Row, 1972, pp. 18–22.

5. Recent research by cognitive scientists in which categories are defined in terms of prototypes rather than in the classical sense of sets with common features is useful here. In this sense, the *dao* is a category that includes roads but takes the waterway as a prototype or "idealized cognitive model." For an exposition of this theory, see George Lakoff, *Women, Fire and Dangerous Things: What Categories Reveal about the Mind* (Chicago: Chicago University Press, 1987).

6. Roger Ames, "Putting the *Te* back in Taoism." In J. Baird Callicott and Roger Ames, ed., *Nature in Asian Traditions of Thought*, Albany: SUNY, 1989, p. 131. Cf. Alvin P. Cohen, comp., *Selected Works of Peter A. Boodberg* (Berkeley: University of California Press, 1979), pp. 460–61

7. See Ames, ibid.; *Shang Shu Tong Jian* 尚書通檢, Gu Jiegang 顧頡剛, ed. (Beijing: Shumu Wenxian Chubanshe, 1982), 06.0084 (九河既道).

8. See Yang Jinding 楊金鼎, ed. *Gu Hanyu tongyong zi zidian* 古漢語通用字字典 (Fuzhou: Fujian Renmin Chubanshe, 1988), p. 426.

9. See Cao Dingyun 曹定云. "*Shi dao, yong jianlun xiangguan wenti* 釋道, 永兼論相關問題," *Kaogu* 1995.11, pp. 1028–35.

10. S.F. Teiser, "Engulfing the Bounds of Order: The Myth of the Great Flood in *Mencius*," *Journal of Chinese Religions* XIII and XIV (Fall 1985 and 1986), pp. 15–44.

11. I have followed the traditional text here, rather than the Mawangdui version; see Chapter 2, note 16.

12. This theme is well developed in later cosmogony. See, for example, the classic formulation in the *Huainanzi* 3/1a, which includes the lines, "In the *qi*-vapor, there was a shoreline. The clear and light rose up and dissipated and became the sky; the heavy and muddy congealed and did not flow and became the earth." For discussion of this passage, see A.C. Graham, *Yin-Yang and the Nature of Correlative Thinking* (Singapore: The Institute of East Asian Philosophies, 1986), p. 30; John S. Major, *Heaven and Earth in Early Han Thought* (Albany, SUNY Press, 1993), p. 62.

13. The Mawangdui manuscripts have 筮 here, a character with the same sound as 逝, which means to divine; but the following line, which refers to going far away, suggests that the Wang Bi editions are correct. See Xu Fandeng, *Laozi Yijie* and D. C. Lau, *Chinese Classics: Tao Te Ching* and Robert G. Henricks *Lao-tzu Te-tao Ching* (London: Bodley Head, 1989), all of whom support this interpretation.

14. Both "configurations" (or images, a term also used for the configurations of the *Yijing* hexagrams) and "things" that I have taken as plural here are more frequently understood as singular, a configuration and a thing—the Chinese does not indicate number.

15. *Tao: The Watercourse Way* (Penguin, 1975), p. 39.

16. *qing* 情 here is taken as *jing* 精; see ch. 4, p. 106.

17. A. C. Graham, *Chuang Tzu: The Inner Chapters*, p. 90 combines these lines with those above into a single passage.

18. The Mawangdui manuscripts are both defective here and so we do not know how this line would have been read. In the Wang Bi edition, the *Daojing* 37 also has the expression *wuwei er wu buwei*, but the Mawangdui manuscripts are different. See D.C. Lau, *Chinese Classics: The Tao Te Ching,* pp. 175–78 for a discussion of the significance of this omission. Gao Ming, among Chinese scholars, has noted that the line *wuwei er wu buwei*, which is constantly quoted in later Daoist literature, may not have been in the original *Laozi*. However, the same sense—that by "doing nothing," the world will be transformed of itself—occurs in other passages (e.g., *De* 16, 57, discussed below).

19. See Arthur Waley, *The Analects of Confucius* (London: George Allen & Unwin, 1938), p. 18, who associates this concept with divine kingship more generally.

20. See A.C. Graham, *Studies in Chinese Philosophy and Philosophical Literature* (Singapore: Institute of East Asian Philosophies, 1986) pp. 59–65. I suspect that the early meaning of this character is the same as *jing* 精, "quintessence." See note 16.

21. *Confucius: The Secular as Sacred* (New York: Harper Torchbooks, 1972).

22. *Disputers of the Tao*, p. 25.

23. *qi qi yan* 戚戚焉, see *Mencius* IIA.2.

24. See A. C. Graham, *Disputers of the Tao*, p. 27. The preposition *yu* (*zhi yu dao*) suggests to me that the *dao* is the course rather than the goal of the movement.

25. *Chuang Tzu: The Inner Chapters*, p. 156.

26. *Zhongguo Wenwu Qinghua* 中國文物清華 (Beijing: Wenwu Chubanshe, 1993), no. 62; see also Chen Banghuai 陳邦懷, *Yi De Ji* 一 徥集 (Jinan: Qi Lu Shushe, 1989), pp. 128–37. The jade is in the collection of the Tianjin City History Museum. Dating relies on the calligraphy and appearance of the jade.

27. Lines that are clearly not arteries are depicted on the body of a lacquered wooden figurine recently excavated from a Western Han tomb at Yongxing, Mianyang County, Sichuan. See He Zhiguo 何志國,

"*Woguo Zui Zao de Renjian Jingmai Qidiao* 我國最早的人體經脈漆雕," *Zhongguo Wenwu Bao*, April 17, 1994. I was allowed to inspect this figurine in August 1994, for which I am grateful to Mr. He Zhiguo. The other lacquer objects from the tomb suggest that an even earlier date is possible. A more complete report by Ma Jixing 馬繼與 is published in *Wenwu* 1996.4, pp. 55–65.

Chapter 4

1. I use the term focal here in a technical sense, by analogy with Brent Berlin and Paul Kay's analysis of color terms in which a focal color—the most intense form of that color—stands for the entire category), see *Basic Color Terms: Their Universality and Evolution* (Berkeley, University of California, 1969). This is an example of the so-called radical effect.

2. See Tao Wang, *Colour Symbolism in late Shang China*, Ph.D. dissertation, School of Oriental and African Studies, University of London, 1993, pp. 89–97; Tao Wang, "Colour Terms in Shang Oracle Bone Inscriptions," *Bulletin of the School of Oriental And African Studies*, LIX (1996), pt. 1, pp. 63–101.

3. See Axel Schuessler, *A Dictionary of Early Zhou Chinese* (Honolulu: University of Hawaii Press, 1987), p. 650.

4. This is what cognitive scientists call a "prototype effect," i.e., all the members of a category are understood to be similar to the prototype of the category.

5. The Mawangdui manuscripts have *tian wu* 天物, but this may be a mistake for the *fu wu* 夫物 of the Wang Bi editions.

6. The *jia* manuscript from Mawangdui has *heng* 恒 rather than the *chang* 常 of the Wang Bi edition (the *yi* manuscript as a lacuna). This may be the original character since *heng* was tabooed as the name of the emperor, Wen, in the early Han Dynasty. In any case, *chang* and *heng* were used interchangeably in the early texts.

7. In the Wang Bi text, these lines are in sections 40 and 42. I have combined them following Xu Fandong, *Laozi Yijie*, p. 61 and the order of the Mawangdui manuscripts. The Wang Bi text has *wan wu* where the Mawangdui manuscript has *tianxia zhi wu* 天下之物, the "living things under heaven."

8. *Disputers of the Tao* (La Salle, Illinois: Open Court, 1989), p. 13.

9. Vassili Kryukov, "Symbols of Power and Communication in Pre-Confucian China: On the Anthropology of *De*," *Bulletin of the School of Oriental and African Studies*, LVIII (1995), part 2, pp. 314–33; Qiu Xigui 裴錫圭, '*Jixia Daojia jing qi shuo de yanjiu* 稷下道家精氣說的研究, *Daojia Wenhua Yanjiu* 道家文化研究, II (1992), pp. 167–92.

10. See Kryukov, p. 316.

11. See Kryukov, p. 321 who translates this term as "perfect virtue"; and Constance A. Cook, "Wealth and the Western Zhou" *Bulletin of the School of Oriental and African Studies* LX (1997), part 1, who translates it as "Corrective Power."

12. See David Nivison, "Royal 'Virtue' in Shang Oracle Inscriptions," *Early China* IV (1978–79), 52–55. but see also Kryukov's rebuttal of Nivison's thesis, pp. 322–24.

13. "Putting the Te Back into Taoism" in J. Baird Callicott and Roger Ames, ed., *Nature in Asian Traditions of Thought: Essays in Environmental Philosophy* (Albany: SUNY Press, 1989), p. 125.

14. See Constance A. Cook, "Wealth and the Western Zhou," *Bulletin of the School of Oriental and African Studies* LX (1997), part 1, for a discussion of the role of cowries as "inalienable goods" in the gift exchanges of the Western Zhou.

15. See Kryukov, pp. 320–21. Kryukov finds the first example of this transformation in the inscription on the Shi Qiang Pan 史墙盤, (*Jinwen Zongji* 金文總集 6792).

16. See A.C. Graham, *Chuang Tzu*, p. 81 for a radical reconstruction of this passage with a much fuller water metaphor taken from Chapters 23, 24, and 7. I have followed the traditional text here.

17. Li Ling and Keith McMahon, "The Contents and Terminology of the Mawangdui Texts on the Arts of the Bedchamber," *Early China* XVII (1992), p. 162.

18. See Qiu Xigui, "*Jixia Daojia jing qi shuo de yanjiu*," pp. 174–82.

19. See, for example, the Shi Qiang Pan 史墙盤: 黃考彌生 (*Jinwen Zongji* 金文總集, 6792, *Wenwu* 1978.3). Compare the *Shijing*, 252 (*Da ya, Juan A)*: 俾爾彌爾性.

20. E.g., Roger Ames, "The Mencian Conception of *Jen Hsing*:

Does it mean human nature?." In Henry Rosemont, Jr., ed., *Chinese Texts and Philosophical Contexts* (La Salle, Illinois: Open Court, 1991), pp. 143–75.

21. Arthur Waley, *Three Ways of Thought in Ancient China* (London: George Allen and Unwin, 1939), p. 205.

22. Harold D. Roth, "The early Taoist concept of human nature," draft manuscript of a paper presented to the Seminar on Oriental Thought and Religion, Columbia University, March 30, 1990.

23. A School of *Zhuangzi* chapter, according to A.C. Graham.

24. "Constant and nameless" is according to the Mawangdui manuscripts; "does not act and nothing is not done," the Wang Bi edition.

Chapter 5

1. See S. Allan, *The Heir and the Sage* (San Francisco: CMC, 1981).

2. John Knoblock, *Xunzi: A Translation and Study of the Complete Works* (Stanford: Stanford University Press), vol. 3, p. 3.

3. I have followed the traditional text here, rather than the Mawangdui version, see Chapter 2, note 16.

4. My working hypothesis in this regard is that *yin/yang* became predominant as technical terms which stand for the system of binary categories through the application of landscape as a metaphor for the body in medical theory.

5. A. C. Graham, *Chuang Tzu: The Inner Chapters* (London: George Allen & Unwin, 1981), p. 156.

6. The parallel with the earliest Greek philosopher, Thales (c. 600 B.C.) who also treated water as the primary stuff has already been made by A. C. Graham. However, as Graham, also points out the "five elements" in China were not constituents of things like those of ancient Greece, but related to the myriad living things by generation rather than composition. Water, too, even in this *Guanzi* chapter, was not so much the constituent of everything as that which generated all the myriad living things. See *Disputers of the Tao* (La Salle, Illinois: Open Court, 1989), pp. 356–58.

Bibliography

Allan, Sarah. *The Heir and the Sage: Dynastic Legend in Early China*, San Francisco: Chinese Materials Center, 1981.

Allan, Sarah, "Shang Foundations of Modern Chinese Folk Religion." In S. Allan and Alvin P. Cohen, ed., *Legend, Lore and Religion in China: Essays in Honor of Wolfram Eberhard on his Seventieth Birthday*. San Francisco: CMC, 1981, pp. 1–21.

Allan, Sarah. *The Shape of the Turtle: Myth, Art and Cosmos in Early China*, Albany: SUNY Press, 1991.

Ames, Roger T. "The Mencian Conception of *Jen Xing*: Does It Mean Human Nature?" In Henry Rosemont, Jr., ed., *Chinese Texts and Philosophical Contexts,* La Salle, Illinois, Open Court, 1991.

Ames, Roger T. "Putting the *Te* Back in Taoism." In J. Baird Callicott and Roger Ames, eds., *Nature in Asian Traditions of Thought: Essays in Environmental Philosophy*. Albany: SUNY Press, 1989, pp. 113–43.

Ames, Roger T. *Sun-Tzu: The Art of Warfare. The First English Translation Incorporating the Recently Discovered Yin-ch'ueh-shan Texts*. New York: Ballantine Books.

Berlin, Brent and Kay, Paul. *Basic Color Terms: Their Universality and Evolution*. Berkeley, University of California, 1969.

Black, Max. *Models and Metaphors,* Ithaca: Cornell University Press, 1968.

Bodde, Derk, "Types of Chinese Categorical Thinking," *Journal of the American Oriental Society*, vol. 59 (1939), no. 2, pp. 200–19.

Callicott, J. Baird and Ames, Roger T. *Nature in Asian Traditions of Thought: Essays in Environmental Philosophy.* Albany, SUNY Press, 1989.

Cao Dingyun 曹定云. "*Shi dao, yong jianlun xiangguan wenti* 釋道, 永兼論相關問題," *Kaogu* 1995.11, pp. 1028–35.

Chan, Alan K.L. *Two Visions of the Way: A Study of the Wang Pi and the Ho-shang Kung Commentaries on the Lao-tzu.* Albany: SUNY Press, 1991.

Chen Banghuai 陳邦懷. *Yi De Ji* 一得集. Jinan: Qi Lu Shushe, 1989.

Cohen, Alvin P., comp., *Selected Works of Peter A. Boodberg.* Berkeley: University of California Press, 1979, pp. 460–61.

Collingwood, R.G. *The Idea of Nature.* Oxford: Oxford University Press, 1960 (first published 1945).

Cook, Constance A. "Wealth and the Western Zhou," *Bulletin of the School of Oriental and African Studies* LX (1997), part 1.

Davidson, Donald. *Inquiries into Truth and Interpretation.* Oxford: Clarendon Press, 1984.

De Bary, Wm. Theodore, Chan Wing-tsit and Watson, Burton, eds. *Sources of Chinese Tradition.* New York, Columbia University Press, 1960.

Eno, Robert. "Was There a High God *Ti* in Shang Religion," *Early China*, 15 (1990), pp. 1–25.

Fingarette, Herbert. *Confucius: The Secular as Sacred.* New York: Harper Torchbooks, 1972.

Graham, A. C. (trans.). *Chuang Tzu: The Inner Chapters.* London: George Allen & Unwin, 1981.

Graham, A. C. *Disputers of the Tao: Philosophy and Philosophical Argument in Ancient China,* La Salle, Illinois: Open Court, 1989.

Graham, A. C. *Studies in Chinese Philosophy and Philosophical Literature.* Singapore: Institute of East Asian Philosophies, 1986. [Reprinted: Albany: SUNY Press, 1990.]

Graham, A. C. *Unreason within Reason: Essays on the Outskirts of Rationality.* LaSalle, Illinois: Open Court, 1992.

Graham, A. C. *Yin-Yang and the Nature of Correlative Thinking.* Singapore: Institute of East Asian Philosophies, 1986.

Hall, David and Ames, Roger. *Thinking Through Confucius.* New York: SUNY Press, 1987.

Hansen, Chad. "Chinese Language, Chinese Philosophy and 'Truth'." *Journal of Asian Studies* XLIV, no. 3 (May 1985), pp. 491–520.

Hansen, Chad. *Language and Logic in Ancient China.* Ann Arbor: University of Michigan Press, 1983.

He Zhiguo 何志國, " *Woguo zui zao de renjian jingmai qidiao* 我國最早的人體經脈漆雕," *Zhongguo Wenwu Bao,* April 17, 1994.

Henricks, Robert G. *Lao-tzu Te-tao Ching: A New Translation based on the Recently Discovered Ma-wang-tui Texts.* London: The Bodley Head, 1990.

Kay, Paul and McDaniel, Chad, "The Linguistic Significance of the Meanings of Basic Color Terms," *Language* LIV (1978), no. 3, pp. 610–46.

Knoblock, John. *Xunzi: A Translation and Study of the Complete Works.* Stanford: Stanford University Press, vol. I (1988), vol. 2 (1990), vol. 3 (1992).

Kryukov, Vassili, "Symbols of Power and Communication in Pre-Confucian China: On the Anthropology of *De*," *Bulletin of the School of Oriental and African Studies,* LVIII (1995), part 2, pp. 314–33.

Lakoff, George. *Women, Fire and Dangerous Things: What Categories Reveal about the Mind,* Chicago: Chicago University Press, 1987.

Lakoff, George and Johnson, Mark, "Conceptual Metaphor in Everyday Language," *The Journal of Philosophy,* vol. 77 (1980), pp. 453–86 (Reprinted in Johnson: 1981, pp. 286–325).

Lakoff, George and Johnson, Mark. *Metaphors We Live By,* Chicago: University of Chicago Press, 1980.

Lau, D.C. *Chinese Classics: Tao Te Ching.* Hong Kong: Chinese University Press, 1982.

Le Blanc, Charles and Blader, Susan, eds. *Chinese Ideas about Nature and Society: Studies in Honour of Derk Bodde.* Hong Kong: Hong Kong University Press, 1987.

Li Ling and McMahon, Keith, "The Contents and Terminology of the Mawangdui Texts on the Arts of the Bedchamber," *Early China* XVII (1992), pp. 145–86.

Li Xiaoding 李孝定, *Jiagu wenzi jishi* 甲骨文字集釋, Taipei: Institute of History and Philology, Academia Sinica, 1965.

Lin, Paul J. *A Translation of Lao Tzu's Tao Te Ching and Wang Pi's Commentary,* Ann Arbor, Michigan University Press, 1977.

Loewe, Michael, ed. *Early Chinese Texts: A Bibliographic Guide* (*Early China Special Monograph Series,* 2), Berkeley: Institute of East Asian Studies, 1993.

Ma Jixing 馬繼興, "Shuangbaoshan Han Mu Chutu de Zhenjiu Jingmai Qimu Renxing" 雙包山漢墓出土的針灸經脈漆木人形 *Wenwu* 1996.4, pp. 55–65.

Major, John S. *Heaven and Earth in Early Han Thought: Chapters Three, Four, and Five of the Huainanzi.* Albany: SUNY Press, 1993.

Mote, Frederick W. *Intellectual Foundations of China.* New York: Albert Knopf, 1989.

Munro, Donald J. *The Concept of Man in Early China.* Ann Arbor: University of Michigan Press, 1977.

Munro, Donald J. "The Family Network, the Stream of Water, and the Plant: Picturing Persons in Sung Confucianism." In *Individualism and Holism: Studies in Confucian and Taoist Values.* Donald J. Munro, ed., Ann Arbor: Center for Chinese Studies, University of Michigan, 1985, pp. 259–91.

Munro, Donald J., ed. *Individualism and Holism: Studies in Confucian and Taoist Values.* Ann Arbor: Center for Chinese Studies, University of Michigan, 1985.

Needham, Joseph. *Science and Civilization in China,* vol. 2: *History of Scientific Thought,* Cambridge: Cambridge University Press, 1956, reprint 1972.

Needham, Joseph, *Science and Civilization*, vol. 3: *Mathematics and the Sciences of the Heavens and the Earth*. Cambridge: Cambridge University Press, 1959.

Nivison, David, "Royal 'Virtue' in Shang Oracle Inscriptions," *Early China* IV (1978–1979), pp. 52–55.

Pepper, Stephen C. *World Hypotheses: A Study in Evidence,* Berkeley, California: University of California Press, 1970 (originally published in 1942).

Postgate, Nicholas, Wang Tao and Wilkinson, Toby, "The evidence for early writing: Utilitarian or ceremonial," *Antiquity* LXIX, no. 264 (Sept. 1995), pp. 459–80.

Qiu Xigui 裘錫圭, "*Jixia Daojia jing qi shuo de yanjiu* 稷下道家精氣 說的研究," *Daojia Wenhua Yanjiu* 道家文化研究, II (1992), pp. 167–92.

Richards, I. A. *Mencius on the Mind.* London: Kegan Paul, 1932.

Richards, I. A. *The Philosophy of Rhetoric*, Oxford, 1936.

Rickett, W. Allyn (trans.). *Guanzi.* Princeton: Princeton University Press, 1985.

Rong Geng 容庚, ed., *Jinwen Bian* 金文編 , Beijing: Zhonghua shuju, 1985.

Rosch, Eleanor, "The Structure of Colour Space in Naming and Memory for Two Languages," *Cognitive Psychology* III, pp. 337–54.

Rosemont, Henry Jr., ed. *Chinese Texts and Philosophical Contexts*. La Salle, Illinois: Open Court, 1991.

Roth, Harold, D., "The early Taoist Concept of Human Nature," unpublished paper.

Sacks, Sheldon, ed. *On Metaphor.* Chicago: University of Chicago Press, 1978.

Schuessler, Axel. *A Dictionary of Early Zhou Chinese* (Honolulu: University of Hawaii Press, 1987), p. 650.

Schwartz, Benjamin I. *The World of Thought in Ancient China.* Cambridge, Mass.: Harvard University Press, 1985.

Shima Kunio 島邦男. *Inkyo bokuji kenkyū* 殷墟卜辭研究 (Tokyo: Kyuko Shoin, 1971), pp. 188–216.

Teiser, S. F., "Engulfing the Bounds of Order: The Myth of the Great Flood in *Mencius*," *Journal of Chinese Religions* XIII and XIV (Fall 1985 and 1986), pp. 15–44.

Tu Wei-ming, "The Continuity of Being: Chinese Visions of Nature," In J. Baird Callicott and Ames, Roger, eds., *Nature in Asian Traditions of Thought: Essays in Environmental Philosophy*, Albany: SUNY Press, 1989.

Waley, Arthur, trans. *The Analects of Confucius*. London: Allen and Unwin, 1938.

Waley, Arthur, *Three Ways of Thought in Ancient China* (London: George Allen and Unwin, 1939).

Waley, Arthur. *The Way and Its Power: A Study of the Tao Te Ching and its Place in Chinese Thought*. London: George Allen and Unwin, 1934.

Wang, Tao. *Colour Symbolism in Late Shang China*, Ph.D. dissertation, School of Oriental and African Studies, University of London, 1993.

Wang Tao, "Colour Terms in Shang Oracle Bone Inscriptions," *Bulletin of the School of Oriental and African Studies*, LIX (1996), pt. 1, pp. 63–101.

Watts, Alan. *Tao: The Watercourse Way*. Harmondsworth: Penguin, 1975.

Whitrow, G. J. *Time in History*. Oxford: Oxford University Press, 1988.

Yan Yiping 嚴一萍, *Jinwen Zongji* 金文總集, Taipei: Yiwen Yinshuguan, n.d.

Yang Jinding 楊金鼎, ed. *Gu Hanyu tongyong zi zidian* 古漢語通用字字典, Fuzhou: Fujian Renmin Chubanshe, 1988.

Zhongguo Shehui Kexueyuan 中國社會科學院, ed., *Jiaguwen Bian* 甲骨文編, Beijing: Zhonghua Shuju, 1965.

Zhongguo Wenwu Qinghua 中國文物清華, Beijing: Wenwu Chubanshe, 1993.

Zhou Fagao 周法高 et al, ed., *Jinwen Gulin* 金文詁林, Hong Kong: 1975.

Chinese Texts

Citations of Chinese texts are to the following editions:

Guanzi Zuangu 管子纂詁, An Jingheng 安井衡, ed., Taibei: Heluo Tushu Chubanshe, 1976.

Han Shu 漢書, Beijing: Zhonghua Shuju, 1962.

Huainan Honglie Jijie 淮南鴻烈集解, Liu Wendian 劉文典, ed., Beijing: Zhonghua Shuju, 1989.

Laozi Yijie 老子臆解, Xu Fandeng, 徐梵澄, ed., Beijing: Zhonghua Shuju, 1988. (n.b., this edition numbers the *Dao* and *De jing* chapters separately. The *Daojing* chapter numbers correspond to those of the traditional text chapters. For citations from the *Dejing* of the *Laozi*, I give the *Dejing* chapter number as assigned by Xu Fandeng, followed by the chapter number(s) of the traditional text order).

Lunyu Yizhu 論語譯注, Yang Bojun 楊伯峻, ed., Beijing: Zhonghua Shuju, 1980.

Mengzi Yizhu 孟子譯注, Yang Bojun 陽伯俊, ed., Beijing: Zhonghua Shuju, 1960.

Mozi Jiangu 墨子間詁, Sun Yirang 孫詒讓, ed., Taibei: Heluo Tushu Chubanshe, n.d..

Shang Shu Tong Jian 尚書通檢, Gu Jiegang 顧頡剛, ed., Beijing: Shumu Wenxian Chubanshe, 1982.

Shi Ji 史記, Beijing: Zhonghua Shuju, 1959.

Shijing Jizhu 詩經集誅, Zhu Xi 朱熹 , ed, Hong Kong: Guangzhi Shuju, n.d. (n.b., this edition does not number the songs, but I have cited the numbers given in the *Concordance to Shih Ching*, Harvard-Yenching Institute Sinological Index Series, supplement no. 9, Peking, 1934).

Shuowen Jiezi Gulin 說文解字詁林, Ding Fubao 丁福保, ed., Beijing: Zhonghua Shuju, 1982.

Xunzi Jianshi 荀子簡釋, Liang Qixiong 梁啓雄, ed., Hong Kong: Zhonghua Shuju, 1974.

Zhong Yong 中庸, Shanghai: Commercial Press (Sibu Congkan 四部叢刊), 1919.

Zhou Yi Quan Jie 周易全解, Jin Jingfang 金景芳, Lu Shaogang 呂紹綱, ed., Changchun: Jilin Daxue Chubanshe, 1989.

Zhuangzi Jishi 庄子集釋, Guo Qingfan 郭慶藩, ed., Taibei: Heluo Tushu Chubanshe, 1974.

Index of Translations of Chinese Texts

Index of Chinese Terms

ben 本: root, source, origin, 36, 71

bu zheng 不爭: to not contend, 47–48, 82, 139. See also *zheng*

cai 才: first shoots of a plant, seedling, natural endowment, original material, potential, 109, 111–113, 120, 126–27, 134

cai 材: first shoots of a tree, timber as a raw material, natural endowment, original material, potential, 110, 111–113, 120, 126–27

cao 草: grass, herbs, straw, wild plants, 15

chang 常: constant, constancy, encompassing a continuum of regular changes, regularity, 98–99, 141, 145. See also *heng* 恆

da 達: to break through, to come out, to penetrate, 59, 69

dao 道: way along which people move, such as a water-course, path or road, channel, natural course, method, natural order of the world, that which is amorphous and ineffable, the Way, 26, 37, 40–41, 65, 66–78, 125–26, 128, 132, 134, 137–38, 144–46

to cut channels, to guide, to lead, to guide along channels, antecedent to *dao* 導, 68–70, 74

to speak, to tell, 69–70

dao 導: to guide, to lead, to conduct, 68–69. See also *dao* 道

de 德: potency, favor, gift, grace, sexual favor, inner power, inner vitality, mana, virtue, 66, 70–71, 83, 101–106, 113, 121, 127, 129–30, 135, 139, 143–44

di 地: earth, 21

di 帝: ancestors in the main line of descent, 20

duan 端: emergent shoots, sprouts, 86, 113–14, 134

171

fa 法: law, 50
fei 非: negative particle, not be-
longing to the category of,
what is not, wrong, 16, 86

gen 根: stalk, to be rooted, 135
gui 歸: the movement of a tributary stream toward a
larger body of water, to
move toward, to return to,
to return home, to turn to,
to give allegiance to, 43–
44, 47, 71, 80, 86, 121, 132–
34, 137

heng 恆: constant, constancy,
encompassing a continuum
of regular changes, 99, 143
hua 化: to change, to transform,
117
hun 昏: chaos, confusion, murk,
the mixing of two sub-
stances—one clear and one
dense, 76
hun 魂: ethereal soul, 37

jian 堅: hard, 81
jian 鑒 (監): vessel filled with
water, 51
jiao 交: intercourse, 45
jing 精: semen, sexual fluids,
essence, quintessence, 88,
106
jing 靜: still, stillness, 46, 53, 83,
98, 117, 140–43
jing 鏡: bronze mirror, 51
junzi 君子: son of a lord, gentleman, 70, 106, 129

lei 類: type, species, 109
li 力: power, 139
li 利: to benefit, 47, 74
li 禮: ceremony, rites, ritual
propriety, 20, 67, 70, 82,
114, 129

ling fu 靈府: spiritual store-
house, mind/heart, 113
liu 流: stream, to flow, 50

meng 萌: sprout, 97
ming 明: clear, bright, 53
ming 命: order, command, gift,
mandate, seasonal pattern,
continuum of regular and
constant changes in the
natural world, natural
order, 98, 104, 108, 113,
134–35, 141, 144–46 See
also *tian ming* 天命

ni 逆: flowing outside a course,
unchannelled, going against
the flow, 91–92
ning 寧 (濘): dense, muddy, 76

po 魄: corporeal soul, 37
pu 樸: "uncarved block," unworked timber, natural
state, 120–21
pu 璞: jade as crude rock, 120–21

qi 氣: breath, clouds, mist, water
vapor, cycle of water which
nourishes all life, ultimate
life force, energy, vitality,
vital spirit, 26, 60, 65, 86,
87–92, 110, 116, 125–26,
144–46
qiang 強: strong, 81
qing 青: color of grass and other
living plants, green, grey,
shades of blue and black,
cool wet color, 15–16
qing 清: clear, 76, 140
qing 情: natural endowment
(Warring States texts);
emotions, passions (Han
Dynasty), 85
qu 取: to take, to draw a principle from, 3, 35, 50

wu 無: to not be there, to not
  have, there is not, to be
  without, nothing, 72, 75,
  79–80, 142
wuwei 無爲: doing nothing, without action, without willful
  action, 24, 26, 48, 65, 78,
  79–85, 87, 105, 115–16,
  120, 126, 138–40, 142–43

xia liu 下流: lower reaches, 47
xiao 孝: filial piety, 20
xiaoyao 逍遙: free of conscious
  deliberation, to roam freely,
  roaming, to wander, wandering, 83
xin 心: mind/heart, 25–26, 53, 65,
  83, 85–87, 102, 109, 126
xing 性: potential contained by a
  seed, qualities with which
  one is endowed at birth,
  that which is inborn or innate, human nature, nature,
  14, 42, 81, 102, 107–11, 115,
  117–19, 127, 129, 134–35
xiu 修: to adorn, to cultivate,
  cultivation, 105–106
xu 虛: empty, empty of sediment,
  53, 84
xuan 玄: dark, 105, 142
xue 學: to learn, 85

yang 陽: southside of a mountain, top of a mountain;
  sun, fire, bright, light,
  above, male, 58–59, 142,
  147
ye 也: grammatical particle indicating a copula (to be,
  belong to the category of),
  15–16
yi 義: rightness, sense of right
  and wrong, 110, 114, 118

yin 陰: north of a mountain,
  south of a river; moon,
  water, dark, darkness,
  below, female, 58–59, 142,
  147
you 有: to be there, to have,
  there is, something, 72,
  75–76, 79, 142
youwei 有爲: doing something,
  84, 143
yuan 原 (源): fount, spring,
  source, 50
yuan 淵: deep spring, abyss, 76

zai 在: to be at, to be in, 75
zheng 正: straight up, correct,
  perfect, to correct, to rectify, 102, 140
zheng 正: to contend, to contest,
  47, 139. See also *bu zheng*
zhi 之: to go, 86
zhi 志: cognate of zhi 之, to set
  one's mind/heart upon a
  certain course, intention,
  will, 71–72, 86, 90
zhi 知: to be intelligent, to have
  understanding, 55
zhi 直: straight, 103
zhi 智: wisdom, 114
zhi 植: to plant, 103
zhi 稙: to sow, 103
zhu 注: irrigation channel, watercourse, to make a channel,
  40, 74–75
zhun 準: carpenter's level, standard, moral standard, 34, 53
zhuo 濁: muddy, 76
zi 自: self, 115
ziran 自然: to be so of itself, that
  which is so of itself, natural, nature, spontaneity,
  spontaneous, 14, 77, 115–
  17, 127, 140

Subject Index

abstract concepts, 9–10. *See also* metaphor, root metaphor
derived from analogy, 13
grounded in natural metaphor, 4, 25, 31, 65
acupuncture, 36, 57, 74–75, 126
agriculture, 46, 48, 65, 81–82, 131, 145
Ames, Roger, 17, 68, 102–103
analogy, 3, 11, 45, 74, 102, 115. *See also* metaphor, root metaphor
abstract concepts derived from, 13
argumentation by, 23, 42
ancestor worship, 18, 19. *See* ancestral spirits
ancestral lineage
individuals in, 101, 106
like continuum of plant reproduction, 12–13, 19–22, 99, 126
linking spirit world to living, 22, 106
ancestral spirits, 20–22, 34, 88. *See also* nature spirits
animals. *See* birth, death, maturation, reproduction

birth metaphor of, 12, 99–100, 108
categorized with plants, 5, 12, 22, 27, 74, 86, 95, 100, 130
man distinguished from, 119
Analects, 6–7

benevolence. *See* humaneness
Bible, 4, 18, 47. *See also* creation myth
birth, 12, 98–100, 108, 117. *See also* generation, of all living things; initial beginning. *See also under* animals
blood, 87, 89, 92, 123, 132
blooming, 126. *See also* flowering, maturation
Book of Songs, 36, 51, 106
brain, 85–86. *See also* mind/heart
Boodberg, Peter, 63, 68
bronze inscriptions. *See under* Zhou Dynasty
brotherly devotion, 71
Buddhism, 86, 98, 129, 148

cartography, traditional Chinese, 35

modeled on plant imagery,
111, 127
reputation as lacking, 36
natural order, 12, 25, 37, 44, 46,
75, 79, 97–99, 108, 113, 130–
31, 134–36, 141, 144–45
nature spirits, 19–20, 55. *See
also* ancestral spirits
Neolithic times, 19
Newton, Sir Isaac, 11

oracle bone inscriptions. *See
under* Shang Dynasty

plants. 4–5, 81, 95–96, 140. *See*
blooming; death; flower-
ing; fruit, bearing of; generation; reproduction;
seed, dropping of; seed-
lings; shoots; sprouts. *See
also* animals
categorized with animals, 12,
21, 74, 96, 99, 102, 108
growth of, 6, 10, 13, 55, 71,
89, 97–98, 110–11, 115, 144
rainwater revives, 65, 92
reproductive metaphor of, 12–
13, 20, 100
pond, 76, 78, 85, 87, 65, 105,
126–27. *See also* still water
pool, 86–87, 142. *See also* still
water
predestination, 98, 130

qi gong, 87
Qin Dynasty, 6
Qiu Xigui, 102

rain, 31, 39, 44, 59, 88. *See also*
clouds
controlled by spirit world, 20
has no source, 3, 36, 65, 71
fills irrigation ditches, 3, 31, 36
from mist, 92, 126

reputation associated with, 3–
4, 36
sprouts watered by, 109–10,
132–33
reason, 85, 93, 96. *See also* mind/
heart
religious tradition. *See also* Buddhism, Confucianism,
Daoism
Greek, 4–5, 18–19
Indo-European, 4–5, 18, 22
Judeo-Christian, 4, 11, 18, 39,
100
reproduction. *See also* ancestral
lineage; fruit, bearing of;
seed, dropping of
plants continuum of, 12, 20,
99–100, 102, 126
requirement of the filial son, 99
reputation, 3–4, 36, 101
rhetorical technique
analogy as, 23, 42–43
rightness, 24, 43, 49, 91, 117–18
rites, 19–20, 50, 67, 70, 82, 89,
91–92, 129
ritual practices, 18–20, 22, 82,
114. *See also* ancestor
worship
mirrors of water in, 34, 51
mountains and rivers in, 54
rivers, 29, 31–35, 39, 43, 50, 58,
77, 79, 132
carry detritus downriver, 46,
50–51, 65
channeled, 39, 41, 68, 71, 73,
75, 80, 125, 130
flow east in China, 23, 35, 39,
134
gentlemen stare at, 9, 11–12,
23–24, 32, 36, 50, 81
paired with mountains, 20–
21, 54–57, 142
takes the lower position, 45–
46, 54, 75, 121, 143

178

Made in the USA
Middletown, DE
12 January 2024

47768601R00110